BOURGEOIS · SYLVAIN DAIGLE · CEDRIC MORIN · LINDA LALLIER · DENIS HAREL · ROBERT DUFORT · JEAN MARC A FERLAND · STEVE M GOUPIL · STEPHANIE L RENAUD · PAUL R ROZON · DENIS ST-GERMAIN · ANDREA M EASTMAN · GAETAN FORTIER · NORA
G HILTON · NORMAND LACOSTE · MAUREEN G HOME · JACQUES GIGUERE · FRANCOISE RAINVILLE · CHOQUETTE FRANCOIS · MARC LONGCHAMPS · ANDREW RETCHLESS · FRANCOIS PHANEUF · JOSEE LAMONTAGNE · BLOUIN MARIE FRANCE · ANGELA
MARTIN · BRUNO M ROY · RACHEL E HOSTETLER · TIMOTHY N MACKEY · MARYSE THERRIAULT · BRETON SEBASTIEN · PATRICK GOSSELIN · JEAN-MARC BENARD · PASCAL AUGER · YANICK VINCENT · ANDRE GUIMOND · MARYSE LONGCHAMPS · **DAY 23** ·
NANCY DAVIGNON · GILLES MARTIN · PAUL JR DESHAIES · MARTIN C DORAIS · ANDRE VIGER · RACHEL DRAPEAU · JIMMY GAGNE · JACQUES NADEAU · MARTHE TANGUAY · FRANCISCO J PINERO · HENRI WATIER · LISE LAFLEUR · DANIEL DRASSE · LINDA M
CHRISTENSEN · GERALD GILBERT · STEPHANE HAMELIN · ANDRE JR HARDY · LORI A KITEALA · ANDRE LACHARITE · SILVAIN LAROUCHE · SHEILA J MACLEAN · THOMAS R MATTHEWS · MICHAEL MOLINER · LIETTE PITRE WES ·
LUC DOHERTY · SERGE NOLLET · JEAN-SEBASTIEN RIEV · SUZANNE TETREAULT · ANDREA BLACKWELL · JAMES A BLOUIN · JOHANNE BRUS · MARIE-EVE SINOTTE · SUZANNE E SAVOIE · MAXIME B OGER
TIMOTHY H CLAYSON · LINDA CALUORI · PATRICK DESAUTELS · SEAN J HORNE · JOELLE N LESCOP · RICHARD MONETTE · JENEIFER L MATHEIS · ROGER L PAGE · MEGAN L POWELL · JAMES P GR ARS ·
LUC ROUILLARD · CHRISTINE M DUCOLON · DONALD BASTIEN · DOMINIQUE MORIN · CHRISTIAN HARVEY · SONIA QUATTROCIOCCHI · DENYS HUOT · NATALIE ROUSSEAU · FRANCOIS BEAUL RGET
NANCY THERRIEN · JACQUES LAVOIE · PIERRE C MOSER · GUY VEILLEUX · JUDITH HARVIE · ERIC JACQUES · MICHEL R KUPIN · COLLETTE CARDIN · DANIEL LAMBERT · RICHARD LAURENC LET ·
CASSONDE YVON · MYLENE CHARTRAND · GUY LEHOUX · PASCALE VINET · CAROLYN WOOLGAR · JEAN LAVOIE · NORMAND LALONDE · MICHEL HEBERT · HELENE P PAQUET · DANIEL SAINT BIENVENUE ·
MARIO DESAUTELS · CHRISTOPHER J ANDERSON · MATTUZZI GINNY · SEAN A HARRISON · NORMAND CHOQUETTE · SHEILA D HUBER · RICHARD J GOULET · BENOIT GUILBERT · CAROLE BELANG JR MARQUIS · LOUIS-PHILIPPE RUEL · HELENE
PAQUETTE · GLENN A SHEWCHUK · DANIEL THEBERGE · BARBARA A RAYMOND · THIVIERGE JEAN · SOPHIE I POIRIER · PATRICK FOUCAULT · GUILLEMETTE MAXIME · HELENE LESSARD · RICHARD PLANTE · LISE ROBIN · GERARD COTE · LUCIEN JOLIN · BRIAN C
PEARCE · DERAPS HUGUES · JEAN-CLAUDE LEMIEUX · ROCH ROULEAU · KARINE DUPUIS · PIERRE CAPLETTE · CLEMENT CHARLES · CARAYANNIS GREGORY · MANON MENARD · SEBASTIEN F FARKAS · BENOIT LESAGE · JEAN-CLAUDE MESSIER · GILLES VACHON ·
DAVE L BURGESS · MARC ANDRADE · MICHEL AUBE · GENEVIEVE BERUBE · MARIO L BLANCHET · VINCENT E CHENIER · MANON DAUPHINAIS · JASON N CUROTTE · LAWRENCE E LYTH · COUTURE LUC · GILLES PROTEAU · LINDA ROUX · GUY PETITCLERC ·
EAN SAURIOL · VALERIE BOUCHER · MARTIN BOURDUA · RENAUD P PIRSCH · JEAN CHOQUETTE · MANON L NOEL · JUAN G PEREZ · ROBERT W KIRNAN · PIERRE LAMY · BENARD N TANYA · FARID TANNOUS · PIERRE USEREAU · HOLDE H TIARKS · YVES
BEDARD · DIANE DAVID-NEVEU · JIM D NEWIN · JEAN DEMERS · LESLIE J AITKEN · SIMON DUCHESNEAU · JUANITA GARZ · DENIS J FOURNIER · LOUISE GOYETTE · JEAN-LOUIS LEMIEUX · JENNY A LAREAU · ALFRED LAPOINTE · JACQUES F SKUTEEKI · JENNIFER L
HACKBUSH · REAL QUINTIN · CHRISTINE OSTIGUY · DON A TARDIO · GABRIEL KEITH · JEAN-PIERRE GUERTIN · LOUISE CASAVANT · MATTHEW GIBB · FRANCOIS CHOLETTE · MARIE-CLAUDE BAITHAZAR · GHISLAIN SCHINCK · FREDERIC LAROSE · CHERYL
MACKAY · MICHEL RICHARD · MARTIN SCULLY · JEAN PIERRE BEAUVAIS · JOSEE BOUCHER · LUC CHAMPAGNE · CATHY FOURNIER · JOANNA COLLINGE · YVES DESROSIERS · DIANE GORECKI · LORRAINE JANIGA · MICHEL COUTURE · MICHELE LEVASSEUR ·
PATRICK ROCH · FRANCOIS GAGNE · MARTIN GINGRAS · BRIAN KELLY · DIANE LEGARE · **DAY 25** · CARMEN ARCHAMBAULT · ROGER GOYETTE · CHANTAL FERRON · PIERRE GAUVREAU · MANON METIVIER · PETER A ALBANO · MONA DITCHAM · DAVID G
MCCALLUM · TERRY L WILSON · SEAN W MOORE · GISELE C CUNNINGHAM · MAURICE CORMIER · JOEL M BONN · MARC VAN ERUM · KARL G GARZ · WILLIAM E O GARZ · PIERRE AUCLAIR · SILKEN LAUMANN · DANIELLE LAUMANN · RACHEL LAMARRE · LISE
GOULET · CLEMENT LANOIX · KRISTINA D KNOPP · CLAUDE A LEONARD · SOPHIE MAJEAU · SHAWN W MATTON · JENNIFER L MERCIER · EDMUND`S MERCIER · MARIE LAVOIE · DENIS PIANAROSA · GINGRAS MIREILLE · RICHARD R REGIS · YVON RIENDEAU ·
VALERIE THIBAULT · DOUGLAS T VAILLANCOURT · CATHERINE VALTON · JEAN FRANCOIS VANDRY · GENEVIEVE BELEC · CHRISTIAN COLLIN · ISABELLE BOUCHARD · STE CROIX STEVEN · MARTINE DOYON · MAURICE J D'AMOURS · ROBERT DUBE · DANIEL
FAGNANT · PIERRE J FRANCOEUR · ALYWIN MORRIS · MARCI KAWENNANORON DELISLE · GINO-LOUIS J HAREL · GILLES HOSSON · ROBERT LAPALME · ANTONIO DUMAIS · RACHELLE LABERGE · KEVIN A KEEGAN · CRAIG W MILLER · GERARD J DESROCHERS ·
ROGER PILON · ALLISON V HAYDEN · BRUNO LEPINE · EGON A LEU · JOHN D MATHESON · CAROLE MILLETTE · MICHAEL R MORIN · RONALD R MURIA · SONIA PICARD · WILLIAM PLESKO · ROBERT PRIMEAU · WILLIAM A PURDY · DENIS SAINT-PIERRE · JOHN
C SLAVICH · LISE SURPRENANT · SERGE TRUSSART · MARIE JOSEE DUBORD · PAUL VERONNEAU · CLAIRE VIGNOLA · HERMAN DELISLE · IAN F GOODWIN · BLAINE LECKETT · JEAN MARC LEROUX · STEPHEN B LUSSIER · YURY I MONCZAK · NELSON ROBERT ·
PIERRE TOUCHETTE · GREGORY R NEWSOME · BILL V MANG · LAWRENCE S OSTOLA · DOUGLAS R LION · MARK W TOBIN · JOHANNE VALLIERES · NICOLAS BARBEAU · PAUL H ENROS · GESCHE E SCHIMMELPFENG · PIERRE J FORGET · ELIZABETH D EVANS ·
DOUGAL MACDONALD · DAVID P RAFAL · LOUISE VERMETTE · PIERRE GENDRON · LOUIS G ROLLIN · MARIANNE UTIGER · YVES LEROUX · ANDRE ADRIEN J LAPOINTE · **DAY 26** · MALCOLM D PRESTON · RICHARD DANJOU · ISABELLE MERCIER · EDMUND A
DZIAK · PETER SCHLEICHER · GUY FARAND · JEAN-PIERRE THOUIN · GENEVIEVE CHOLETTE · BRIAN R HOWARD · MARIO A JOLICOEUR · CHARLES L MILOT · PAUL A VANDENYSSEL · JON D CHATTERSON · LUTHER CARVER · CATHERINE L MOSCO · DOUGLAS
ANAKIN · VIC EMERY · JOHN EMERY · PETER KIRBY · NANCY P STEWART · JOSEPH FORNAROLO · MARNI E BRYDON · LORNE FRIEDENBERG · LESLIE A HAY · SHAWN M HAMILL · PATRICK R MURPHY · JUAN-CARLOS PECA · JOSEE LANOUETTE · STEVEN W
WHEELER · ROBERT VOTTERO · MARC AUBIN · KAREN C DEROCHE · ERIC BRAULT · GREGORY J BUIE · MARK G BEASSE · JANICE P SANSOM · ROBERT N LISTER · SIMON SAUVE · WAYNE A SYVRET · DOREEN H STEIN-SACKS · LAURENT THIBAULT · LEONARD
WILLETT · IAN AITKEN · RAYMOND CHADI · IAN R HODKINSON · CAROLYN DAVIES · SONNY CROTEAU · JEFFREY AK DICK · BENJAMIN ELIASOPH · ANDREW J CASSOLATO · LYNE ST LOUIS · DONALD A FARRELL · HAROLD L FISHER · MICHAEL A GARBER ·
SUSAN IRVINE · MARC LAMPRON · BRIAN C MOSHER · FAY L KRISTENSEN · BRIAN W MURPHY · WALTER RASCHKOWAN · ZOE N COWIE · DEREK L ROLSTONE · YANICK ROSE · GUY RUEL · MANON NADEAU · FRANCIS A TOURILLON · RICHARD R CHIASSON ·
NELSON RIOUX · PIERRE CARPENTIER · STEPHANIE PETREMENT · TONY CIORRA · FRANCOIS F HARDY · DOMINIQUE L JAMET · SUZANNE LAROCQUE · JEAN J JOLY · CARON LOUIS · DANIEL MORIN · YVETTE Y O'KEEFE · MICHEL PAQUIN · ANDRE PARE · PATRICK
PERLUZZO · CHANTAL DESROSIERS · PATRICK SAUVE · SIMON GELINAS · FRANK PORTOLESE · JACINTHE SYLVAIN · PIERRE TURGEON · DAVID J TURNER · SYLVIE VIOLA · **DAY 27** · KATY PETTIGREW · LORTIE PIERRE · SYLVAIN DIOTTE · PATRICK LAFLEUR · MIKE
LEVESQUE · ROMEO U BASTIEN · ADRIEN BLOUIN · GUYLAIN G ROY · CHANTAL BAIRSTOW · GUY J CHATEAUVERT · JOYCE G M LY · JOSEPH ALBERT MARIO WINTER · DOUCET AMELIE · SERGE CAMPEAU · RICHARD BERNARD · MARIE BARRETO · MICHEL
CHARLEBOIS · JEAN HUOT · MINA SCIANNAMBLO · EMANUEL MARTORANA · ANNE MATTE · SERGE MARINEAU · SUZANNE S OUELLETTE · LAURENT CUTTER · MARIE-PIERRE CARDINAL · JEAN-PIERRE DAOUST · YASMINE CHIDIAC · MICHEL DRAPEAU ·
CHANTAL CLAVEL · RICHARD FOUCREAU · CAROLINE CORNELLIER · MARY C COWANS · MARIANA A FRANK · PHILIP AMALFI · JANE M O'DOWD · MICHEL KENTZINGER · LEANNE M BACCHIOCHI · FRANCISCO M HERNANDEZ · ALLAN MICHEIL INNES · ROBERT
MACDONALD · STEVE MAINVILLE · PATRICIA MARTIN · RICKY MARTIN · D BRUCE MCKINNON · PIERRE ST JEAN · ANDRE SIMARD · SYLVIANE SEGUIN · FRANCINE C POISSON · MARTIN R SCHILLER · MONIQUE ST-CYR · EMILY L HARARI · JEREMY A SELWAY ·
NICOLE A MATTHEWS · NICOLAI SCHNEIDER · PAOLINA TESTA · CHRISTIAN THU-THON · GILLES TROTTIER · JOSEE TURCOTTE · DOMINIC J VINCELLI · NATHALIE VAILLANCOURT · RICHARD M WYGANOWSKI · RITA VISSANI · CARL J ANDERSEN · NORMAN L
BELLEFONTAINE · DANIEL LOISELLE · STEVE LESSARD · MARIO MIELE · DANIEL J AUCOIN · KELVIN J BERRY · MARTIN-PIERRE BOULIANNE · ROBERT BURNS · LAURIE C CARTMAN · ERIC DELLIERES · SYLVIA CORBETT · MARC GARCIA · LOUISE C FONTAINE ·
CHRISTIAN SICARD · NATHALIE MARCEAU · ROBERT N BERLETTANO · BARBARA ANN SCOTT · ALEXANDRE HEBERT · ROGER GAGNON · SABINE S DEFILIPPO · MARTIN LAROCQUE · ORI DROR · CATHERINE LEDUC · ANDRE VILLENEUVE · ALAIN PRENOVEAU ·
NATACHA M TENDLAND · DAVID W HOOPER · KENDRA A GRIFFITHS · TARAS MS PAWLOWSKY · CHRISTINE A JONAS · MARIANNE E NIOSI · GARY R RICHARDSON · HENRY ROSENHEK · ROGER J ROY · SILVA A SARKISSIAN · VIET-CUONG PHAM · LINDA J
STADELMAN · NEIL BERG · IVY L STEINBERG · STEPHANE ASSELIN · ELYSE GUILMETTE · PETER F SPIERENBURG · LUC GREGOIRE · **DAY 28** · HELENE PAQUETTE · MICHEL DURACEAU · HUGH P THOMASSIN · RHONA WURTELE GILLIS · NORAH E GOOD · GAYNOR
A PRIESTLEY · PIERRE VILLEMAIRE · BARRY J BELLWARE · JOSEE CARRIERE · THOMAS STEPPAN · JACQUES A LE BER · MICHAEL T ZEAGMAN · RIMMA N LAZZAROTTO · KARL-ROGER BOURASSA · LUC COTE · MARIE-CATHERINE BERNARD · SYLVIE CHARRON ·
FRANK M BLACKWOOD · DAVID BOBALJIK · NANCY GRIFFITHS LANTHIER · FRANCIS BOIVIN · MICHAEL S BOYLE · SYLVIE E BRUNELLE · SYLVAIN CHOQUETTE · HELEN ORA COHEN · FRANCOIS I COLLIN · GUY LEBLANC · IAN F CRAWFORD · COLIN H DAY ·
BRIGITTE DESROCHES · LINDA-ANN M DI DOMENICO · JULIE DUTRISAC · BILLY FRANTZESKOS · URBANO FUMAGALLI · NICOLAS GIRARD · MARK D GOLDENBERG · NATHALIE GOUPIL · EDWARD R TURPIN · ISABELLE BELEC-PLOURDE · DEBORAH GROSS ·
FRANCOIS HETU · CRAIG R HUTCHISON · JENNIFER R HUTCHISON · RICHARD LAGACE · ROBYN ISRAEL · JEAN-BRUNO LATOUR · WAYNE SPOONER · CLAUDE LECAVALIER · RICHARD LOISEAU · SEBASTIEN LORMEAU · MICHEL NORMANDIN · PEPIN YVES ·
MARIO POCE · KATHLEEN E BROOS · CAROLE ROUSSEAU · JEAN ROUSSELLE · MICHEL ROZET · MICHEL SARRAZIN · PATRICIA M SEELEY · WILLIAM J SCULLION · RONY BIANCHI · ANGELA CUTRONE · ROBERT J BARCLAY · CHANTAL ARSENEAU · MARC LORTIE ·
RAYMOND BELISLE · CLEMENT SROUR · JANE K TRAKALO · SEBASTIEN CAMPION · EVELINE GAGNE · BRIGITTE N MAYES · MARTINE DAGENAIS · STUART H LACEY · IRIS IRONS · LOUIS VANIER · JAMES VAN RYSWYK · MICHEL BROUILLARD · DENIS G FONTAINE ·
DENA M THEBARGE · ANDREW K HUGESSEN · DAVID A LOWE · MARTIN VIAU · **DAY 29** · MADELEINE M CODERRE · LUC GAUTHIER · JAMES E LYNG · ROGER R BERGERON · DANIEL CLAVEAU · MARK C SMALLHORN · MAUREEN L DESROCHES · TARA J MATTICKS
JEFFREY ADAMS · DANIEL T ALBRECHTSON · ELYTON H ARMSTRONG · GEORGE A BALL · REJEAN BASTIEN · ANDRE A BOILY · JULIE DOMINICK · GEORGE SHORT · BRYAN W TODD · KEITH J FULLARTON · STEPHANE GAGNON · LOU A KOZELJ · GERALD
LECLERC · THOMAS LEISHMAN · PATRICE P CHARLEBOIS · SCOTT A ABELSON · MARILYN G WEIR · ROBERT KALNINS · JOACHIM H TIARKS · ISABELLE RIVERIN · JULIE J THOMPSON · MAURICE CHARRON · GERALD BOUCHER · ROGER ARCHAMBAULT · ROXANNE
AYOTTE · JOHN J MOSCO · MARC DESJARDINS · SERGE S PAYANT · MONICA G BRUINSMA · DENIS D CLOUTIER · GILLES J VAILLANCOURT · MICHAEL M RAPOSO · GREG J ZOBATAR · MARIE ANDRE PAQUIN · ROBERT ORMOND WRIGHT · JENNIFER E
MCNAUGHTON · PHILIPPE A TELLIER · ROCH CARPENTIER · ANNIE A COURSOL · RUTH R DESCHAMPS · SYLVIE GODIN · ROBERT I SETO · TONY E ROTHERAM · ERIC E PATTIN · RENE P SINGH · KEVIN K COULOMBE · DANIELLE A APPLETON · PAUL MONGEON ·
FORTIER DENIS · BRIGITTE LANOIS · JAMES E HURD · MARIE-JOSEE L LEHHOUX · YVON Y PATRY · PETER J PRIBIL · JACQUELINE MADILL · DAVID WEBB · MICHEL R LAFRAMBOISE · JEAN-PIERRE DE BEAUMONT · SARAH WHEELOCK · FRANCINE D CECIRE · MARTIN
PLOUFFE · DENIS D BEAUDOIN · MARC-ANDRE VACHON · GUY S BRUNET · STEPHANE L DEMERS · ELISABETH G VAN EYKEN · SERGE MELOCHE · DANIEL ROZON · NORMAND J THERIAULT · ERIC FORTIN · LUC GIROUARD · CAROLE DUPONT · SEBASTIEN
LAUZON · SYLVAIN SIMARD · SONIA ROY · PIERRE LACROIX · ROGER DUCHAINE · CLAUDIE EMOND · **DAY 30** · KAREN F DOUGLAS · KRISTI A LAMBERT · JOHN A GRUBER · LINDA JACKSON · LANCELOT R BENNETT · ARON BARRETT · LORNE M DEAN ·
GRAHAM D EAVES · SEAN A CLANCY · ALVIN H BLOOM · TODD D BRABANT · ANNE C BRADLEY · FRANCIS M REED LANG · DARYL C MACPHERSON · JOLANTA E MILLER · MISS CATHY A SCOTT · JUDY ZELMAN · SUSAN M KOLAR · GARY T HALL · MICHEL ADAM
JAMES M FRASER · REBECCA P KAUFMAN · DAVID H MORROW · LAURIE T CANTIN · A PETER CLELFORD · TOM C CRABTREE · LOUIS A BERGERON · MAX DEAN · GEORGE C LAIGHT · JAMES M CLOUTHIER · GARY M HOWARD · LAURIE M GOLDMANN · KAREN
HOGAN · MICHAEL P LECLAIR · JOEL RIOUX · LEANNE M ECHLIN · DR IAN ZUNDER · PHILLIP A VOLPE · MICHAEL R NOEL · JENNIFER BELFORD · MARY C MACLENNAN · JOE E MARCEAU · MICHAEL J SOUTHGATE · DAULTON THEODORE · LESLEY J PAMPARARO ·
JEAN-CLAUDE PERRAS · CAROLYN J MOORE · BENOIT L MAINVILLE · MARC LECLAIR · KENNETH E MAUGHAN · IRVIN TAYLOR · FRANK DUNSTER · TED HIBBERD · ORVAL GRAVELLE · REG SCHROETER · ALBERT RENAUD · PATRICK GUZZO · ANDY GILPIN ·
MURRAY DOWEY · ANDRE LAPERIERRE · WALLY HALDER · ESTELLE D ESSEX · SANDY WOOLEY · RICHARD BEECROFT · CHRISTOPHER S SMITH · GLENN A ROBERTS · STEWART M RISTO · SEAN P ALLEN · JOHN J DEMARCO · GISELLE L FLEMING · ANDRE DORVAL ·
CATHERINE E POTTS · DAVID J MAYMAN · CAROL-ANN SHUTRON · STEVEN M JOHNSTON · JOSEE BERTRAND · FRANCINE CLEMENT · DANIEL J MCCARTNEY · ANNA M PROVICK · ROBERT C REYNOLDS · GERTRAUD E VOGEL · ELAINE WILLCOCK · SUK KHUAN K
UM · FRANCE M LAROSE · SUZANNE M JANELLE · ROBERT F GERARD · DEBRA M GRANTHAM · MARGARET L HYNES · ANNE E LEWIS · KIM A POWELL · MARTIN P BRASSARD · KRISTINA L SNIDER · CORINNE CHENIER · GREG POPOFF · ALLISON JONES · KEN
MACLEOD · LARRY HEGAN · DAVE HOLLINGSWORTH · **DAY 31** · CAROLE K DUCHESNE · BRUCE MACCALLUM · ALLYSON ROSSITER · WAYNE A REED · J ANDREW TONNER · LARRY ABRAMS · LAURA L BEAUDETTE · STEPHEN K VETTER · ANDRE O AYOTTE ·
SONIA MOREAU · ROBERT J BOURDEAU · GARY SANDERSON · RALPH A POFFENROTH · GINETTE BERTRAND · BRYAN G BAKER · JOHN B BOISCLAIR · DANIELLE BROUILLET · NORMAND E BRULOTTE · KAREN BALL · CAROL PILON · STEPHEN J TAMAS · ALLAN J
TAVERNER · JEANNETTE OUIMET · ROBERT K LOOS · CLAUDE LAROUCHE · DIANNE LABELLE · ROBERT W BOUGH · TOM E TODD · GEORGES R BOUGIE · MARYANN CURRIE · GEORGE C MOFFATT · SUSAN A TANTALO · SHELDON W HARRIS · LORNA M
DRISCOLL · ROBERT A HICKS · SHANNON M HIEMSTRA · JOSEPH J KROL · ROXANNE FORTIER · LORRAINE L HUTT · DAVID G PIDGEON · DOUGLAS W SAVARY · MARK NADON · LISA L LANGEVIN · MARTIN J SCHOONES · MARILYN A WADE · ROBERT
STANDRING · PRISCILLA L WATSON · HENRY J ZWIREK · RANDY J TYRRELL · NICOLE M VAN WYLICK · KATHY KREINER · ROBERT LALONDE · RON J HIPFNER · SUZANNE A ROSE · MARIA E THOMPSON · KARL U TROMMESHAUSER · JULIE E CULL · HEATHER K
NAFTEL · DAVID A BOWMAN · LYNNE H ALEX · MURRAY H CAMPBELL · ROBBIE S DOIG · PATRICIA L SOCHASKY · ROBERT G GOLLINGER · SANDRA L GUMMESON · EARL W GUMMESON · BEVERLEY J LAWSON · RUDY MADSEN · DAVID E MALKIN · CAHL M
POMINVILLE · DAN A ROY · CORY A ALLAN · RICHARD G COVILLE · TONYA BENNETT · RHONDA EDMOND · TIMOTHY M EGAN · RONALD D GAUTREAU · CYNTHIA A GREER · RICHARD D HALL · LIISA R JAAKKIMAINEN · FRED KELLEY · SHELLEY E LUPTON ·
LARA S PLAISTED · ROBERT MACKAY · JOAN M MACKINNON · TRACY A MEEKER · CLARENCE WRAY · JENNIFER WILSON · SAMANTHA L MASON · TRINH THI PHAN · CLAUDINE NADEAU · JAN PEACHEY · BARRY DE GRAY · DAVID W DUFFY · JASON E DUFFY ·
DAY 32 · LARRY F MEEK · JULIAN A DONALD · JO WELLS · DOUGLAS C ALLPORT · PATRICIA E DAVIDSON · ROY K BROOKS · BONNY MAXINE FERGUSON · SHAWN K GLADU · WILLIAM A INGRAM · JACK M MAILLOUX · RAY CISLO · CATHERINE S EADY ·
DONALD M GLOVER · JIM R GORDON · AYNSLEY POMINVILLE · PETER C HENRY · BEVERLEY F MANEELY · STEPHEN MILLER · JAYME A O'REILLY · JEANNETTE M FROESE · MARY V SHAW · JAMES T ELLERTON · HEATHER J DEIR · REG G FREEMAN · RUSTIN M
HOLLYWOOD · SUSAN J COUPER · ALLAN T REID · BRIAN SUTTON · DAVID M MACDONALD · DR G A TAYLOR · RON J POIRIER · PRESTON S SCHIEDEL · DIANE SOULE · KARIE ARMSTRONG · GAYE B BECKWITH · CAROL A CARTIER · STEVEN M BLACK · ELANOR
M CIRTWILL · NEAL A COOPER · MYRA K CORCORAN · HELEN LOFTIN · JAMES CORCORAN · JUDITH M DASILVA · AUBREY FLETCHER · ANNE M FERGUSON · NORMAN S HART · ALEXANDRA D FLORIAN · LINDA THOM · FREDERICK L JARDINE JR · RICHARD
DAVISON · BRONWEN M COX · PAULA L MACKENZIE · TRACEY L MALLEN · JEFFERY D MANN · DAVID H WILSON · DONNA E PETERS · MARK R OWEN · PATRICK J Y MENARD · IRENE MEAGHER · JAMES SHELDON · CHRIS A STEEVES · PATRICIA L TAVARES · JOSEPH
A MARSHALL · GARY W MCPHIE · GUY H TOWNEND · TROY D SPETZ · KEITH D SINE · RICHARD N PAPI · HOWARD A SANDLES · JOHN STEINBACHER · ROBERT PHELAN · PAUL PRIMEAU · RUTH RALPH · LIETTE D LEMIEUX · CLIFFORD BROOKS · MATTHEW
MENARD · ROBERT NW BABCOCK · REBECCA JOHNSTONE · BILLY J OFFICE · JOE MCNAMARA · BRYAN LAMBERT · BRENT FORREST · TYLER RIDER · COLIN TAYLOR · SCOTT HAINES · **DAY 33** · ROBERT D RENOY · RUDI A FLINTERMAN · DARREN L CHAPMAN ·
VICTORIA L EDGE · WILLIAM H OOSTERHOLT · KAREN M BROWN · BRYAN C GREER · SHANNON L O'ROURKE · HENRY A JANZEN · ROBERT J HUNDT · LARRY A LAMB · DEBRA WOODWARD · MURRAY J WALLER · CLAYTON R PHILLIPS · JAESON E LECUYER ·
LAURIE J WINTER · ANTOINETTE MONGILLO · ALEC J DENYS · ANDREW A CLAPPERTON · DANIEL R COLLADO · CHARLOTTE A ROSENBLATH · DOUGLAS A SCOTT · GREGORY N BRANT · TARA K MCLAUGHLIN HALSEY · ROGER R CORBIN · MARGARET J
BATEMAN · HARRY DANFORD · BARBARA E BOOS · DANIEL N DESMARAIS · SHEILA M DAY · BRYAN P DILTS · SHARLENE A HOLDEN · NICHOLAS R FRY · KAREN L IRELAND · MARILYN D BUCHOLTZ · ANNE E HITCHON · SCOTT MARACLE · GARY A ITO · DAVID J
JEFFREY · MELODY W KISS · BERNARD LOEFFLER · JULIE-KAY LANG · DAVID G MOCON · JERRY W REID · STANLEY T OSBORNE · DAVID N PALMER · ALASDAIR G PATERSON · JOHN D PUDDY · ROBERT S SOLMES · ERIC M TAYLOR · GARY P TWEEDY · TERRI A
VAUGHAN · STEPHEN P WALLER · MARGARET P BERRY · PERCY G BRADLEY · ELIZABETH M BONGERS · WILLIAM C BRUNDIGE · CATHERINE A CHERRIER · JIM L CLARKE · ANNE DUNHAM · WILLIAM R ELLIS · SANDY B HALLIDAY · ANN J HUSSEY · PETER H
KENNEDY · JOHN H LANSING · ROBERT PAUL · BARBARA W HOFFMAN · CATHARINE M GARRAH · CHRISTOPHER A LEEDER · EDWARD J MCCOLM · JASON T MENAUL · NANCY C MOORE · GREGORY D ROGERS · MELANIE FOX · JOSS TREMBLAY · KELLY L
ACKROYD · JOHN T BACON · CATHY A BAKER · ROUEL Q BARRANDA · CARA R AMOR · JOE COLASURDO · JOE A CONNOLLY · ANNE P FLOYD · VALERIE A THIBAULT · DAVID P HOWE · ANDREW D COOK · PATRICIA A GENOE · RANDY P KIMLIN · MARK T
EDWARDSON JR · JANET E GIBSON · MICHAEL C JAMIESON · SPENCER G LAVIS · DONNA MARASTON · MURRAY A LIVELY · PHIL A MYERS · BRENDAN A MATTHIAS · LEIGH F NOLAN · GEORGE A SCOTT · HEATHER L MILLARD · JOHNNY VAG JR · MIKAL A
HISCOCK · ALICE M DESLAURIERS · WENDY A DESLAURIERS · RAVI SRINIVASAN · MARK ARSENAULT · SUE STAPLE · **DAY 34** · KAREN M CLOSS · ROBERT L CROWE · FRANK W HARVEY · DAVID J INCH · DAVID LIPNOWSKI · ALBERT G MIDDLETON · JAMIE E
NEWTON · DOUGLAS D NURSE · GERAID D O'KANE · ELAINE L ROSS · DAVID B ROSS · MICHAEL R PARTRIDGE · JOE A SANDOR · RAUL AGOSTO · LINDA M BARKER · TRACY L BEAVER · JODY L BEVAN · DANIEL J BULGER · GLADYS M DELONG · JOHN M DAVIS ·
MARCI F EDWARDS · WILLIAM R GOODWIN · PETER J GREATHEAD · CRAIG B GRAY · JOHN W INGLIS · GREGORY L KUMPULA · RICHARD F MADDIGAN · JOHN F MADDIGAN · BRUCE A PATTERSON · TANYA A RAYMOND · BARRY A SKITCH · DARLENE C COPOC
JOHN WOOD · PAUL STATHAM · ROBERT D HAMILTON · KATRIN RUDERT · KEVIN O MCCANNY · JOHN BARDELL · RUDOLF C BRAAT · TERRY J MCNULTY · ROBERT B PHILLIPS · GRAHAM A TYE · SUSAN L BASKERVILLE · CRAIG R BEATTIE · DAVID J CHALLICE ·
MIKE E BUKOWSKI · PAUL D CHARLTON · ALLISON CAMPBELL-ROGERS · HENRIK DAMSBAEK · SHARON E CREECH · ANDREW M FLOOD · JODIE A DONALD · BOB GALLAGHER · TROY FARRELL · LAUREL K GALT · ARON J FINN · LARRY GILLMAN · JOANNA G
HAGERMAN · JOHN T GROWDEN · KAREN D DUSOME · MICHELLE L HENDRIKS · STEVE R HILL · LOUISE P INNES · IAN R JEFFERY · WILLIAM J (BILL) LANOUETTE · AMY L JUNKIN · VELJO LAUR · LYNDA M LEADER · JOHN G LEISHMAN · JEFFREY M LIVINGSTONE ·
BARBARA M MARSH · ADAM W MATTHEWS · JOSEPH S MAXINE · RONALD J MCFARLAND · LISA D MCGILVRAY · DAVID G MEEKIN · GLENN PECKOVER · LORI J PENEYCAD · TODD D ROBERTSON · KATHRYN L LINTON · SARAH RUSH · DEBORAH A SACCOCCIA ·
FREDERICK E SMITH · WILLIAM L ROGERS · RUTH L WHITNELL · KENNETH J TEDFORD · SHERRY L TELFORD · DARREN E WARBURTON · JOHN D WILLIAMSON · BROOKE N MCARTHUR · BRAD RUSAW · DAVID LAPOINTE · DAWN NIGRO · PETER MASEE · **DAY 35** ·
VALERIE A MCLAUGHLIN · LARA BEATTY · LES GILSON · MIKE T ROGERS · CHRIS ALLINGTON · RICHARD D HESLIP · ROSELYNE CAMPBELL · RODERICK A NAILER · JOHN R ROBINSON · SCOTT A MERTON · CATHIE L FICKLING · CATHERINE A BARRY · TIM
WILLIAMS · CRAIG MCLAUGHLIN · TONY HEAYN · STEPHEN E BURROWS · JASON L BEATTY · KIM J CHAMBERS · EILEEN G ISAAC · ELLA M MCRAE · GARY W MITCHELL · EUGENIE WOLSEY · HEATHER A SALZMAN · KARL W ARMSTRONG · SHERRY L PROUTY ·
BARRY T KING · ROBERT A ROUGHLEY · STEVE H BARRY · ANDREW J BRUCE · K ALISON CHASCZEWSKI · SONNY LEE · PETER DOPPING · DAVID E JONES · MICHELLE P MARDER · JOHN C MACKINNON · BARBARA M MORTON · JOHN F REID · MICHELLE H
ROBICHAUD · LARRY D SILK · TROY B SHARPE · DEBBIE J THOMPSON · ROBERT G COLLINS · MARK C TANNER · JENNIFER M TILK · HUGH G ALLEN · MARK A ALLISON · SONIA M ARVISAIS · NORMAN J BALL · KATHLEEN A BOYER · THOMAS N CHALMERS ·
NICHOLAS R FORD · AARON E FURGER · GRAY GILLESPIE · MARIA IMBRIGLIO · ROBERT GLEN · ANNE E JORDAN · PHILIP L GRAINGER · LYNNE A MACDONALD · GORDON A HAMPSON · NANCY G MCGREEVY · MARION E CHAMBERS · MELISSA A HARTY ·
FREDERICK HOLLAND · NICOLE E MOUNTAIN · ROBERT D PATTERSON · LINDSAY M NOLAN · BRIAN PETER · SHANE E O'NEIL · BOB J BELL · SYLVIA RALPHS-THIBODEAU · HARRY W RICHARDS · LINDSAY A SIDWELL · NORMAN J RIPPON · MELINDA R SIMPSON ·
BRIAN P STANDING · MARINUS J VANDERMEER · AARON D VANDERMEER · CATHERINE L TURL · MICHAEL J TWINER · NORMAN W VAN-DUYN · BLAINE VARNER · CHRISTOPHER W WALLAGE · PAUL WILLIAMS · LORI WILLIAMSON · PAUL SOUTHWOOD · JOHN
G WEYMOUTH · ANGELA S COLM · GLENDA D O'REILLY · ROBERT J BARRETT · ROB SAFRATA · **DAY 36** · CATHERINE A PARRY · MRS ETTIE A TOEPEL · JOE F DEIDUN · AMANDA G DENNIS · SCOTT B DUNCAN · GORDON R FERGUSON · KIRK A FIGUEIRA ·
CAROLYN P JAMES · TODD D KEAST · BRIAN E LOWES · CORINNE J KUETHER · SUE LUCAS · RANDALL K MOORE · ALICE T MACNEIL · WAYNE PYE · CHARISSA L MORRICE · DONALD JACKSON · NICK P VIRIS · RYAN P SHAW · SHERYL A VERHOEVEN · WILLIAM J
WESTON · JESSICA P STONER · ARNIE J WONG · GAYLE L YETMAN · ROSALIE G BROWN · SUSAN J BEARD · RICHARD A CLEGG · GORDON K CLEE · DEANNA M CIUCIURA · WAYNE FREEMAN · DAVID J STANDEN · NORMAN S GIBSON · KEITH CLARKE · ANDREA L
CROTHERS · WILLIAM G KEARLEY · SHARON L CUNNINGHAM · JASON FEDDEMA · CLAUDE C GONSALVES · MICHELLE P LEBLANC · JOHN HRYNUIK · DEREK A LING · CHRISTINE K MACDONALD · ALVARO J DA SILVA · EMILY A SKLERYK · JIM D COLLINS · MARY
C SLED · MARSHA M MCEWAN · BRADLEY MUNRO · PEN-I SMITH · JENNIFER MCCABE · MAURICE WONG · MYRNA J HENRY · SHELBY E ROGERS · ANITA D LATULIPPE · STEPHEN A HARTLEY · JOHN R BURNS · TIFFANY A BRIDGES · CLARE L CULLEN · RICHARD T
MINETT · ALAN R WHITE · FRANCESCA PERRI · DONALD C TAYLOR · KEITH BRETTELL · JACQUELINE K SAKELLAROPOULOS · BRUCE A WATERS · STEVE SEARS · DIRK HOSTEREY · ERIKA C PIEKE · BARBARA L SELDON · XIAO C ZHANG · **DAY 37** · CHARLIE BELFIORE
DARLENE BOON · BRUNO FILIPPI · DENISE L BURGESS · DENNIS J KOLE · TERRI C SUN · GERALD ESTRIN · DIANA F BEEVOR-POTTS · JOSEPH M FOX · BEVERLY G EPSTEIN · PAUL FREEDMAN · BRENDA L GLENDENNING · RICHARD A GOLISZEK · LESLIE J
GOODYEAR · DAVID J HUNTER · VALERIE I HENDERSON · TIMOTHY J MCCRIMMON · PAUL A LANDRY · ELISA T LIMMER · BEN JOHNSON · ANGELA TAYLOR ISAJENKO · SCOTT A HITCHCOCK · SUZANNE L HIGGINS · EDWARD R REED · SARA J MANN · MARY J
EE · STEVEN J LOFKRANTZ · PATTE MANDEL · STEVE H RIDGWAY · MARY MASTROMARTINO · JOSEPH RODRIGUE JR · MARIANNE L PAMPIN · ANDREW J PATTON · DAVID L WELLNER · KENNEDY D ENG · ANNE C GRIMSDALE · BARB HOTSON · WAYNE C
KAHLAN · LOREEN E KONIG · STEPHEN S KELLY · LEONOR AGOSTO · JOHN MARASTON · MARIE W PRAJZA · GRAEME J LOWIK · HANS W WEICKARDT · MIKO P ROMANO · MICHELE SUTT · JAMIE L LASKOVICH · LAURA A GREENAN · FRANK M MAURY · DAVID R
NURMI · CHRISTOPHER A RAWNSLEY · BRENDAN M PAGET · MELISSA A RICHARDSON · KEVIN R BROWN · GORDON RANSOM · BRIAN L CARR · HAZEL A CROOK · STEPHEN A CARROLL · DONOVAN COOPER · JOHN W HARDING · PENNY WRIGHT · RICHARD
DUNCAN · LAURA MCANUFF · KEITH R GEORGE · MICHAEL P HOLM · ANDREW J GIMBY · ALISON NOBLE · CHAD A MCALPINE · DANNIE A MORRIS · JANIS F MOFFATT · WALT OKIHIRO · PAUL F ROSATO · SUNNI L SCHNEIDER · JACK RICHARDSON · MIKE
STARK · SILVIA A TINTINAGLIA · LAURIE A TUTTE · JULIA A SWEDAK · LINDA S SZARGA · NANCY E CURTIS · ANDREW J EVERTON · LAURA MIRABELLI · JAMES BABINGTON · SUSAN PASSMORE · ANNE GOODWIN · SEBASTIAN ROSA · LESLIE NICOLAI · STEVEN E
GOW · HUGO T SORENSEN · TODD WILLIAMSON · **DAY 38** · IAN R KIDECKEL · JOYCE E ARNOTT · JEFFREY J KRAR · JAY LAURENCE TAYLOR · CHERYL A KEATS · MARK S CABRAL · CATHY M ELLA · DAVID VISSCHEDYK · OTTO JELINEK · MARIA JELINEK · LINDA J
AGG · MATTHEW A THOMPSON · WOLF FROHLICH · JEREMY CREED · MR FRANCIS A HALCRO · MARLENE E KERSHAW · IAN G JOHNSON · JOANNE G LAPENSEE · CAROLYN E LEONARD · MARK W TAYLOR · ANN SINCLAIR · KATHLEEN M WALLACE · TERESA
BOLEY · JOHN R ANDERSON · DAVID G GOEREE · STEPHEN T COPPERTHWAIT · LORI A DAWSON · KENNETH I BROWNE · MARTHA A DONNELL · LAWRENCE E DOW · LISA J VAN DYK · DONALD M MANN · ANGELA L KRUMMENACHER · MARILYN T EDWARDS ·
RODERICK C MORRISON · DALE J ALLEN · LESLIE K EUBANK · JOHN C PHILLIPS · ELIZABETH M GORDON · CARLENE L JENKINS · ROBERT R POLLARD · KAYLEY S LONG · MICHAEL A QUAGLIA · JANINE D TRIPP · KEVIN W SMITH · KELLY J AMOS · MIKE SODER ·
JOHN A O'CONNOR · PETER G STUART · JOANNE ZAWISLAK-TOSELLO · STEPHEN R WRIGHT · LEONARD J WOOD · SHEILA CHRISTMAS · GREGORY W DOWDLE · DAN R HAVERCROFT · KEVIN S HOLLY · DAVID K WHORRALL · ROBET W OLIVE · DANIEL T
WELSH · CHANTAL L TROY · GARY L CHALK · JEFFERY C BOWEN · MARILYN B ARMSTRONG · JOHN FLYNN · MARIE P VILLAMERE · TERENCE N HUTCHISON · RINY H KOOYMANS · ROSS D MANNEN · ALEXANDER J MCQUIRE · TIM F SYMONS · JIM TITMUS ·
RANDALL H VANLAUWE · DIANE D WILSON · ROBERT B NEEVE · JAMES ABBEY · NANCY DIERX · PAUL G DAWSON · GERALDINE NORTHEY · SUSAN E KITZMAN · TRACY R IRVING · DOUGLAS ADAMS · **DAY 39** · DASHA D LUKSICEK · CHRISTOPHER S EVERETT ·
NICHOLAS S RUNDALL · BRANDON KELLNER · RONALD A WARBURTON · MARY J PHILP · MARK YOUNG · VALERIE L LAWSON · MARY L HUMPHREY · JUNE SOWDEN · MICHAEL W HAMILTON · MURRAY W MCEWEN · RON W FLEMING · VINCENT N PEREIRA ·
MICHAEL M JACK · KATHERINE M DEMERS · EDGAR L CLEMENT · RAY MARSH · ALLAN H STANSBURY · JAYNE M RUDOLF · MARK R GILBERT · CHRIS M BLOM · GEORGE PETROVIC · DANA M O'NEIL · JAMIE A CAPSTICK · RICK W THOMPSON · NEIL W HARRIS ·
STEVEN F SLOAN · ADAM D TAYLOR · JANICE E GOODRICH-STEELE · BRIAN D RUSHTON · JEFFERY M BARNES · SANDRA L FALLIS · JASON T CAMPBELL · CAROLYN M KING · SUZANNE L WEBER · DAVID S GREEN · IRENE F CONLON · DEBBIE M BARKER · DANIEL
A WESTBROOK · JOANNE M HOWARD · TREVOR O JOHNSTON · SEAN C MCGRATH · SARAH K DANCAVITCH · PETER W QUINLAN JR · KAREN M MORRIS · JOHN BOYKO · TIMOTHY P WILKINS · DAVID I HURLEY · GERRY D MOAN · WENDY A FOSTER · PAUL W
STRATFORD · ROBERT A PAZZI · TERRY SWANSON · RUSSELL DORRINGTON · CAROLE BERTUZZI LUCIANI · MICHAEL R P DE LA ROCHE · **DAY 40** · KEITH C KINNIBURGH · SHANE D COLEMAN · LESIA M FEDAS · JOHN R PERSICH · DOUGLAS M ALLAN · CHARLES
AMBROUS · ANDREW S ARAI · CHRISTINE E BLYTHE · DONALD E BARTLETT · JOSE M BERNARDINO · RITA BHIMSINGH · SIDNEY H BROOMFIELD · ROSS W ARMSTRONG · NORMAN MILES · HUGH B CAUGHEY · MURRAY R CHRISTIE · GRANT R CLUGSTON ·
WAYNE M EYLES · TONY CONTESTABILE · RENZO R CORSI · DONALD R CRAY · VIRGINIA R DESA · ROBERT J DIXON · NEIL EASTON · WILLIAM R MUIRHEAD · CRAIG H GAY · PATRICE M FODEN · LARRY R GIBSON · PATRICIA E HALL · STEPHEN D GOODGER ·
SHELLEY A HELLEMAN · HARVEY E HUGHEY · TRACEY T HOLLOWAY · JAMIE JARVIE · PAUL E JERVIS · MARTINA L JOYNER · BOGUSTAW W KARP · JAMES M KELLOCK · DEBRA A KING · ALAN D LUTYK · LINDA L MAY · JOHN GALLAGHER · GARY E MOHR ·
PATRICIA M MCSWEENEY · MICHAEL A MOONEY · WILLIAM J MOORE · KIMBERLEY A MORRIS · FRANK S NAGLER · DIANE M NUNZIATO · WILLIAM T PLENDERLEITH · ALLISON S PETRE-TUTT · EARLA J PHILLIPS · LOUIS E POLCI · CHERYL L PORTIGAL · DUSAN D
SATELMAJER · PAUL W SCHAEFER · JEFF A SUTTON · AARON M SZABO · LYDIA ZAHOREC · MICHAEL S ZORATTI · RICHARD P ARSENAULT · DOUGLAS C BANNISTER · JUDY M BRANDOW · LEIGH A ATHERTON · MERVIN H BROWNLEE · JOHN K TROUP · JAMES J
LEMIEUX · MURRAY P BARRICK · PATRICIA J BARAN · LIAM CRAGG · GERARD A EDWARDS · BEVERLEY A HARVEY · ANN BEATTY · ROBERT D MCSWEEN · CYLVIA J POWELL · ERIC NASKALI · RACHEL S RASMINSKY · DR DONALD J URSINO · BRIAN MCMAHON ·
CRAIG A REEKIE · STEPHEN J SULLIVAN · THEODORE C MANGOFF · MARLON R TEE · DAVID W FORREST · DOROTHY J RECEK · SUZANNE E TAYLOR · FLORENCE KUSIAK · GORDON D GOVIER · SHAWN ROCCHI · BILL URCHIK · MIKE MCLAUGHLIN · JEFF
LOCKYER · PAUL HISEM · PETER ARTKIN · PAULA M HUCKO · LUH C WONG · **DAY 41** · NAZIM BAKSH · JACK BOILARD · DARRYL J WILDE · MARK A LANTEIGNE · TIMOTHY L FOLEY · ALISON J ENGEMANN · JACK L MINOR · PENELOPE A DOWNEY · DONALD K
AVERY · LINE S COTE · JAY D COOPER · ROBERT A COOKE · DAVID W BARNES · DEBORAH D ERVINE · GORDON R VANDER GRINTEN · JILL STONEHAM · GREGORY J HAYMES · RICHARD L HERBERT · REBECCA A NIGH · DAVID J PETTY · CATHY M ARCHER ·
ANDREW F ANELLO · BERYL W BAILEY · JOHN C BARILLIER · MARK H COUCH · JACQUE D BOILARD · CURTIS A LEVERE · KEITH R GILLAM · LESLIE MACDONALD · KARLA L BEREZUK · ARTHUR J DOMENICUCCI · CATHERINE M DECOCQ · KEVIN S FERGUSON ·
DREANA K DAWDY · IRENA V CRAIG · ANNE D JOSELIN · MICHAEL E HOEKSTRA · CHRISTINE M JONES · CHRISTOPHER M HALL · CAROL L KELLY · GREGORY G GREGOVSKI · JAMES C GILLIS · DENIS D LAPALME · TIMOTHY A KRAMER · TANYA L LUND · MR
HAROLD P MARQUIS · GINO M VENDETTI · SHARON E KOMSA · KRISTINE M LENAHAN · WILLIAM J MOWAT · TAMMY A OLYNICK · IVAR E NOREN · JOHN A PACSUTA · BRUCE E PIERCEY · PETER G SAHLAS · JAMES K SHIELDS · DEREK M SURKA · STEVE SZABO ·
LINDA L VALDEZ · SCOTT A WINGER · MIKE P AGNEW · ELAINE E ANDREWS · DOUGLAS J BLAKEY · CHRISTINE R ANDRONEY · LUCIANO BONI · WENDY J SHELDON · DONALD L COTTER · STAN J DYMCZAK · SHERRY L FLECK · CONRAD I LIVINGSTONE · GORD
PYLE · ROGER A RUPERT · SYLVIA K STREMLAW · MICHAEL G VRIENS · ANNE L VIVIAN · NICOLAAS T HUITEMA · DOUGLAS I MCLETCHIE · MELVIN C OLIVER · ROBERT B SHOALTS · STEPHANIE L BUCK · ZACHARY ADIE · STEVE J CAREY · MONA L CLARK ·
THOMAS E FORTUNE · JACQUELINE M COLELLO · ALYNN C MEAHAN · FRANK W MCKIBBEN · BRIAN W SMITH · DANIEL S DANIELS · JOHN SIDERIUS · DONALD W GIBSON · STEPHEN G POTTS · **DAY 42** · L SHAWN CLEMENT · KENNETH J ROMAN · JOHN A
ANGER · DAVID E BELME · STEVEN A BOREHAM · MARK A BOSILAC · JENNIFER E CHANDOR · JOE J CONEYBEARE · BLAIR S GERELUS · TRUDY M JARZYNA · BRIAN D LONG · JANICE E LAROSE · GARY A MACDONALD · MELANIE A MORRELL · ROBBIN L PRIDMORE
CATHARINE E PRATT · HEIDE M MUSIL · RAY N SHIRTON · KEITH M SQUIRES · GEORGE W STEPHENSON · JACQUELINE A THERIAULT · PETER L TON · JOHN CVITKOVIC · BONNIE JEAN MCKINNON · PAULETTE A VELSEN · KENNETH C GAZLEY · RYAN W
COUNSBURY · JAMES G NORVAL · SHELLEY L SWIFT · CHRISTOPHER G TEAL · JOHN P BAUSLAUGH · MICHAEL A BISHOP · KATHRYN A COLEMAN · JOSEPH E BLAKE · MARC J CATTRYSSE · JOSEPH R EINREINHOFFER · JOHN MARK W BIRO · KIMBERLEY G HASKETT
JAMIE R HAYWOOD · ORVAL D WILSON · NORMA E HEMSWORTH · ROY N MAIN · MARGARET JONES · CHRISTINE L LOWRY · STAN P PRAPAVESSIS · RICK S SOSTAR · LAJOS SZABO · JOHN W COMERY · RICK A DEBACKERE · SEAN A EBDON · SHERRI L HEFKEY ·
ROBERT M MASSCHAELE · DEBBIE A LOHMANN · JEFF G SAUDER · TARA B RUNGE · PAUL C STADE · BRIAN J VAN ACKER · LORNE A BOYD · SUSAN C CRAIG · RICHARD J NICHOLLS · CHRISTOPHER M BURWELL · BRIAN M COOPER · BRUNO L COSTABILE · PAUL
D BEISCHLAG · WILLIAM R DEANE · RODNEY J FRANKLIN · THOMAS G HILL · PHILIP MONCKTON · JIM J HORVATH · SYLVA SANDRA KUSCH · CARRIE L KONIG · ARTHUR N MACKAY · SEAN W LEWIS · ANDERS NIELSEN · ELKE E POPP · CARL D WILKENS · JAYSON
P YOUCKE · CHRISTOPHER P LESAGE · MIKE WEBSTER · MIKE MILLER · MIKE BLACK · CHRIS CLARKE · MARY C KRESTEL · WENDY B HOWSE · GEOFF CLARKE · SUE RAUSCHER · WADE MONTOUR · **DAY 43** · CHERI LYNN A BRADISH · WILLIAM F BEARD · MARSHA J
ACKLAND · WILLIAM G BERRY · MOIRA J BEVERIDGE · JOHN M CROFT · JANE E CHARLTON · TIMOTHY G HILL · TRACEY L FIRBY · STEPHANIE A DAKINS · GARRY V INNANEN · JILL L HIND · DANIEL R MURRAY · JENNIFER L PICKARD · SYLVIA B LOVE · LARRY F

SHARE THE FLAME

The Official Retrospective Book of the Olympic Torch Relay

No other single event fires the imagination, stokes the enthusiasm and captivates the spirit like the Olympic Games.

The Olympic torch symbolizes the Games' objectives: peace, friendship and sportsmanship. And never before has a country become so involved in an Olympic torch relay. Canadians took part in the 18,000 kilometre odyssey across Canada in the bitterness of winter with enthusiasm, dignity and pride.

Petro-Canada was honoured to have the opportunity, as sponsor and organizer of the event, to bring the Olympics within reach of most Canadians, making participation in an Olympic event a reality. We also viewed our involvement as an opportunity to inspire unity and enhance Canadians' sense of national pride.

Through individual effort, community involvement and cooperation, the country was involved, showing just what can be achieved by Canadians working together.

Under the most punishing winter conditions, Canadians made it happen. From coast to coast, hand to hand, in a remarkable chain spanning the nation, Canadians shared directly in the Olympic mystique and brought the flame to Calgary for the opening of the XV Olympic Winter Games.

For those who struggled against the bitter wind, whether you carried the torch in your hands or in your hearts, you have been part of a journey that showed that the Canadian spirit is as eternal as the Olympic Flame.

W.H. Hopper
Chairman of the Board and
Chief Executive Officer
Petro-Canada

E.M. Lakusta
President and
Chief Operating Officer
Petro-Canada

This book was made possible by the following:

IBM is a registered trademark of International Business Machines Corporation.

Canadian

Xerox Canada Inc.
XEROX

MOTOROLA CANADA

Join Us! Ensemble!

Published by Murray/Love Productions and Whitecap Books

Produced by Murray/Love Productions Inc.
1128 Homer Street
Vancouver, B.C., Canada
V6B 2X6

Distributed by Whitecap Books Ltd.
1086 West 3rd Street
North Vancouver, B.C., Canada
V7P 3J6

Producer/Creative Director: Derik Murray
Director of Operations: Marthe Love
Director of Marketing: Michael Burch
Art Director/Designer: Chris Dahl
Interviewer/Writer: Alan Hobson
Editor: Elaine Jones
Production Manager: David Counsell

Share The Flame was produced exclusively on the IBM Personal Publishing System and IBM PS/2 Personal Systems.

Canadian Cataloguing in Publication Data

Hobson, Alan, 1958-
   Share the flame: the official retrospective of the Olympic torch relay
   Issued also in French under title: Fêtons la flamme.
   ISBN 0-921061-15-3
   1. Olympic torch relay - Canada. 2. Winter Olympic Games (15th : 1988 : Calgary, Alta.).
   I. Title.
GV721.92.H62 1988   796.9'8   C88-091093-3

Printed and bound in Canada.

ISBN 0-921061-15-3

Kharen Hill

Albert Normandin

CONTENTS

INTRODUCTION TO THE OLYMPIC TORCH RELAY

Jim Wiley

The flame that Canadians shared with such fervent emotion on its odyssey to the XV Olympic Winter Games was born far from these shores in a ruined, roofless temple erected by the ancient Greeks to honour Hera, the powerful queen of the mythological gods. Her crumbling shrine stands in the home of the Olympic Games of antiquity, a cypress-shaded archaeological site in Olympia where the first recorded Games were held in 776 BC.

The stories claim Zeus himself once wrestled there, and when the modern Greeks pluck their sacred fire from the sky as they have done at four-year intervals since the ceremony was resurrected in 1936, it is with a nod of respect toward the generations of athletes who won glory and honour on those historic fields.

Flying in the face of superstition on Friday, the 13th of November, a private Challenger jet touched down at Athens International Airport. On board were members of the Calgary Winter Olympic organizing committee and relay sponsor Petro-Canada bearing a special cargo—a gleaming aluminum torch forged in the image of the Calgary Tower.

By November 15, the torch was in the slender hands of Katerina Didaskalou, a Greek-born Shakespearian actress. Within the temple of Hera is a concave mirror aimed at the sun. There the Olympic torch is ignited within seconds by the sun's concentrated rays. That day, the gods were making mischief above Olympia, as cloudy skies threatened to interfere with the vital cooperation of the sun's rays for the flame-lighting ceremony, but two sprigs of fire had been captured

during the rehearsal ceremony on November 14. These had been carefully preserved overnight in miner's lamps; thus the purity of the Olympic flame was maintained.

Accompanied by 14 handmaidens, Didaskalou carried the flame out from the temple to the grove where the heart of modern Games founder Baron Pierre de Coubertin lies buried. There the torch was passed to a Greek runner, who, carrying Calgary's torch in one hand and a branch of olive in the other, launched the relay to Athens. In the Greek capital it was solemnly turned over to an eager Bill Pratt, the president of the Olympic organizing committee.

For the Greeks, the quadrennial ceremony hardly caused heads to turn. They couldn't know the emotional outpouring it would generate on the other side of the Atlantic, as the longest relay in Olympic history unfolded before millions of spectators, or comprehend the logistical planning to guarantee the continuous combustion of that single flame across 18,000 kilometres in a vast land of ice and snow.

Jim Wiley

Jim Wiley

Greg Stott

The relay has its roots in ancient Greece, but it only surfaced in 1936 in what became known as the Jesse Owens Olympics in Berlin. The precise link between the flame and the Olympics is shrouded in Greek history, but the writings of Plutarch describe how glowing embers were carefully preserved within Hera's sanctuary and fanned into flames every four years by victorious athletes, as they carried them to the Games site. In 1936, runner and Games planner Dr. Carl Diem was struck by the idea from ancient Greek drawings and pieced together the details for the first relay, from Olympia to Berlin. It launched a tradition

that has become firmly entrenched in all Olympic planning since, spanning 19 relays, ranging from the 250-kilometre run to Montreal in 1976 to the 15,000-kilometre trek to Los Angeles in 1984.

But the 20th Olympic torch relay to Calgary would set a new standard for those that followed. It would be the longest in distance, covering 18,000 kilometres by land, sea and air, take the longest to complete at 88 days, and move the flame farther north than it had ever been before—above the Arctic Circle.

It would encompass every Canadian province and territory and visit every capital city, coming within a two-hour drive of 24 million Canadians. It would move on foot and by dogsled, snowmobile, helicopter, ferry and aircraft. And it would ignite a cauldron in Calgary's McMahon Stadium at the Winter Olympic opening ceremonies on time, no excuses accepted.

Mass participation from Canadians country-wide became the paramount goal. What the Olympic organizing committee needed was a sponsor to mount the expedition—a sponsor willing to make a multi-million-dollar commitment with limited commercial marketing. That sponsor was Petro-Canada, a government-owned, fully integrated oil company with an exploration division and retail outlets in every province and its head office in the Olympic host city. But nothing prepared the company for what was to come. The magnitude and complexity of the task first became apparent at a January 1987 relay rehearsal.

It was to be fairly low-key, a three-day run through the most rugged terrain the torch would cover on its subsequent marathon. No mass excitement, no tears—a simple test. They were wrong. Hundreds of children lined the route, people gazed in awe at a flame produced by a Bic lighter, the runners called it the thrill of a lifetime. "It was then we knew we had something big," said Ed Lakusta, Petro-Canada president.

The 10 people devoted to relay planning quickly grew to 18 full-time organizers as Petro-Canada prepared to meet its responsibilities. A convoy of 40 cars, vans and motor homes was mobilized, most supplying auxiliary services, such as staging en route ceremonies, providing video production for the media, torch fuelling and

advance crowd control. A staff of about 80 would accompany the torch at all times. It was, Lakusta noted, "the culmination of years of preparation." Planners had covered every step of the relay route with stopwatches and accurate odometers, keeping a sharp eye out for potential problems.

It was decided early that a lottery would be the vehicle for choosing over 6,500 Canadians to carry the flame toward Calgary. By the middle of February, 1987, the biggest lottery in Canadian history was underway. Before it was over, 6.6 million applications swamped two warehouses devoted to the runner selection process. Some entered a thousand times and were picked. Others entered only once and got the call. Most people didn't get that letter giving them a few minutes of glory with the flame in their hands, but no one argued that the system wasn't fair.

It was Baron de Coubertin, in 1896, who set down the guidelines for the modern-day Olympic revival. These words have been written on the scoreboard at Olympic competitions since 1908: "The most important thing in the Olympic Games is not to win but to take part, just

as the most important thing in life is not the triumph but the struggle." Frank King, chairman of the Winter Olympic Games organizing committee, agreed when it was suggested the relay was perhaps the purest form of this vision of Olympic participation. "You can't invent ways to bring people together like this relay. You can't buy the pride it has unleashed. It gives all Canadians a chance to participate in some way."

And so Canadians waited with anticipation for the Olympic flame. Prime Minister Mulroney, who arrived in St. John's on the eve of the relay, said, "It's a great unifying strand across this country. Unity requires a lot more than political speeches. It requires symbols, and the Olympic torch relay is a symbol and a reality of unity."

On that snowy November 17 morning, as a private jet was on final approach to the St. John's airport, carrying the sacred flame in three brass miner's lamps, some thousand spectators prepared to welcome the flame to its final home. Ahead, Canada waited with a million rolls of film, banners, candles, flags and tears.

The Olympic torch relay was about to begin.

—Don Martin

William DeKay

THE MAKING OF THE RELAY

THE REHEARSAL

It might be said that the Olympic torch relay began at the Salmo-Creston Skyway in British Columbia in January, 1987, when Petro-Canada, the relay sponsor, held a rehearsal to learn what they could expect a year later. The company had previously organized a relay that launched the World University Games in Edmonton in 1983, but the Olympic event would be on a much larger scale. The relay manager, with a team of 11 company employees working full time, picked the Skyway because it was the highest pass the Olympic flame would have to cross as it made its way to Calgary. Chosen torchbearers huffed and puffed up the eight-per-cent grade, as Petro-Canada employees ran with them and others observed. What they saw in B.C. led to modifications to the torch, the fuel and some safety procedures, as well as a fine-tuning of the relay organization. It also gave a hint of how popular the actual event would be.

THE LOTTERY

If there were any lingering doubts about public enthusiasm for the relay, they were swept away in the response to the national contest to select torchbearers. In the largest direct-mail campaign ever in Canada, Petro-Canada sent out 10 million brochures. By the contest deadline of March 31, 1987, Canadians had sent in 6.6 million applications. (No one knows exactly how many people participated, because some made multiple applications. A teenaged girl in Manitoba, for instance, is said to have entered the draw 16,280 times.)

After the entries were sorted into 88 bins, one for each day of the relay, a draw, supervised by auditors, picked the runners needed for each day. Applicants were required to specify the day they wanted to run and could choose any section they wanted. Some, by accidentally filling in the forms incorrectly, found themselves running their kilometre far from their homes; others deliberately chose a remote segment of the relay where they might have a better chance to be picked. Still others chose their kilometre for sentimental reasons, returning to their home towns, where friends and relatives could help celebrate.

THE TORCHBEARERS

The lucky torchbearers—approximately 6,500— ranged in age from 4 to 86. They included husbands and wives, entire families, women who would give birth just before or just after their run, people in wheelchairs, people with pacemakers, people in the pink of health and others recovering from life-threatening illnesses. Some ran, some walked, some rode in a wheelchair, snowmobile or dogsled.

Three hundred other torchbearers were selected in the designated category outside the lottery. Physically and mentally challenged people, nominated by handicapped associations, were picked in a draw. Kilometres were set aside for non-Status Indians and Native Canadians. Past and present Canadian Olympians were invited to participate and were picked in a draw, and some others were chosen for their contributions to their country.

All torchbearers were closely followed by an escort runner, charged with ensuring their safety. About 150 Petro-Canada employees, tested for their physical fitness, shared this task in shifts of six to eight days.

THE TORCH

The crafting of the torch required the services of companies in Quebec, Ontario, Alberta and British Columbia. The process started in Calgary, where Petro-Canada employees conceived a torch bowl reminiscent of the landmark Calgary Tower. Prototype torches were developed by the National Research Council in Ottawa, and a Calgary firm was chosen to handle the job. Certain tasks were subcontracted: the handle, of Quebec maple, was turned on a lathe in Calgary; the pictograms, representing the 10 Winter Games sports, were burned into the handle by an Edmonton firm; the fuel container, which was formed of specially hardened steel from a Vancouver distributor, was engraved in Windsor. The finished torch measured 60 centimetres and weighed 1.7 kilograms.

The fuel, which burned for about 45 minutes in the torch, was developed by Petro-Canada. The research team blended gasoline, kerosene and alcohol, eventually creating two combinations to meet a variety of weather conditions and indoor use.

RELAY UNIFORMS

The torchbearers wore track suits that became instant collector's items. The red and white suits, with the relay emblem front and back, were made in Winnipeg

Kharen Hill

and Calgary, using a lightweight, breathable material. On their heads, torchbearers wore white acrylic, fire-retardant toques. Runners supplied their own shoes and gloves. The uniforms, tagged with each runner's name, were shipped under security across the country, where they were safely stored until handed out at one of the daily briefing sessions to the eager torchbearers.

THE CARAVAN

The torch crossed Canada accompanied by a caravan of about 40 vehicles and a rotating crew of some 80 people, made up mostly of Petro-Canada employees. Seven vehicles stayed with the torch: a police cruiser led the way; a motor home carried torchbearers, dropping them off at one-kilometre intervals as their turns came; the lead car bore two miner's lamps burning with the Olympic flame, to relight the torch should it go out; a large media truck, open at the back, held photographers and reporters from national and international media, and was usually positioned in front of the torchbearer; behind the torchbearer was the command centre motor home with relay officials, escort runners and medical crew; a van to pick up torchbearers came next; and the last car was a police cruiser.

The caravan's other vehicles carried supplies, torches and fuel, stage equipment, a mobile film-editing studio with satellite up-link, snowmobiles, and Hidy and Howdy, the Olympic mascots.

LOGISTICS

Part of Petro-Canada's detailed planning involved making sure that everything would be in place as the caravan moved across the country. Each day hotel accommodations had to be confirmed for an average of 80 crew members; 225 meals were ordered; locations for briefing of media, staff and runners were booked; supplies ranging from communications equipment to coffee were shipped to places where they would be needed; the torchbearer track suits were shipped; and transportation was arranged so that crew members could be rotated.

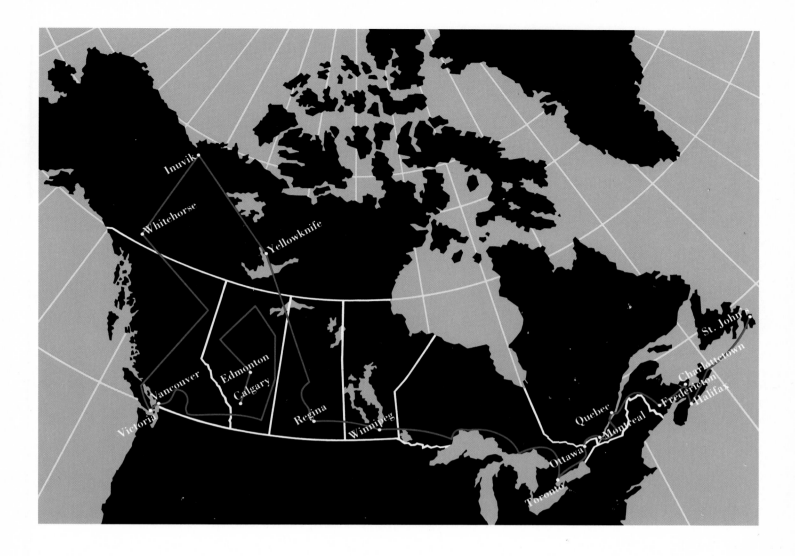

THE ROUTE

Following a route that had been test-driven three times, the Olympic flame zig-zagged 18,000 kilometres across the country, on secondary roads when possible. It travelled 11,000 kilometres on land, and 7,000 by airplane, helicopter and ferry. Starting at Signal Hill, Newfoundland, the torch headed west by foot, transferring to snowmobile for 2,750 kilometres, from Shanty Bay, Ontario to Prince Albert, Saskatchewan. Sitting behind a driver, each torchbearer held the flame for 15 minutes. When the torchbearers in a group had all completed their turn on snowmobile, they ran as a group for one kilometre, handing off the torch to each other. At Saskatchewan the torch took to the air, flying north to the Northwest Territories and the Yukon, and then south to British Columbia. On B.C.'s Vancouver Island, runners continued the trek east to Alberta, where the flame went by foot and plane before reaching Calgary on February 13.

The torch travelled on 89 calendar days, but because it started and ended at midday, it was officially considered to have taken 88 days. It visited 800 cities, towns and villages, including the capitals of the provinces, the Northwest Territories and the Yukon, and it came within a two-hour drive of 90 per cent of the population. It stopped for some 400 community ceremonies, where medallions supplied by the federal government's Celebration 88 program were presented to people who had demonstrated the Olympic spirit in their communities. Olympic downhill skier Jim Hunter hosted these ceremonies, accompanied in Quebec by diver Sylvie Bernier. The stages, lights and sound equipment were supplied and set up by the relay project team as it progressed across Canada.

THE BOOK

This book follows the relay as it proceeds across Canada, and is structured around the 88 days of the relay and its route, outlined on the map above. Each section of the book begins with a locater map, which details the part of the route covered in that section.

Something was astir in Canadians on those winter days when the Olympic torch crossed the country. Something pulled them out of their warm homes, to stand in the cold, waiting for a runner, holding the flame that symbolized so many things. Some, it is true, came to cheer on a son, a wife, a grandfather, a friend. Some came to see former Olympians or favourite athletes. Some came to touch the maplewood handle of the torch, to think that for a moment they had been one with the sun-born fire of Olympia.

All these things brought Canadians to the side of the relay road, but something transcendent happened to them there. They found that their friends, their neighbors, their sons, daughters, mothers and fathers, were links in a chain of heroic people strung across the winter-blasted country. They realized they lived among heroes, among winners, among people of vision and strength. They saw that they could do what had never before been done so efficiently, so graciously, so hugely.

Something caught fire in these reputedly fire-resistant people. They burned with pride for their local runners, for their tiny towns, for their great nation. They ran out of their houses and shouted to the passing cavalcade, "We love you, Canada." They stood in their high school gyms and their public squares and they sang their national anthem with newly glowing hearts.

This book is about that record-making relay, about the eager people who carried the torch, about the way they work and live, and about the country that inspired their love. But there is an underlying story here—of a self-contained people opening up, saying to the world what they have seldom said so surely before, that they are imaginative, proud, strong, free. And that they are united in cherishing what makes them unique. This book is dedicated to those people.

A FLAME IS KINDLED
Newfoundland, Nova Scotia, Prince Edward Island, New Brunswick, Day 1—15

From downtown St. John's on Duckworth Street, keeping the harbour on the right, you climb Signal Hill. There is a small lake here, George's Pond, and Cabot Tower, where Guglielmo Marconi received the first trans-Atlantic wireless message. But what is impressive about Signal Hill is its austerity. There is no difficulty here in understanding why Newfoundland is called The Rock. This is where on November 17, 1987, the first torchbearers set off to carry the Olympic flame, a kilometre at a time, to the Winter Olympics in Calgary. If the place to begin anything is at the beginning, Signal Hill and St. John's are that, geographically and chronologically.

It was in 1583 that Sir Humphrey Gilbert, with a charter from Queen Elizabeth I, sailed into St. John's Harbour under the brow of Signal Hill, and laid claim in her name to the land around. Even then, he was a latecomer. It was John Cabot, a Venetian serving Henry VII, who discovered what he called the New-Founde-Land, sailing its coast in 1497. The English sailors in Cabot's crew brought back wondrous tales of fishing grounds so rich that a basket weighted with a stone would do as well as a net.

Soon, French, Basque, Spanish, Portuguese and English fishermen were making annual voyages. Indeed, the sheltered harbour at St. John's was filled with French and Portuguese ships as Sir Humphrey proclaimed Elizabeth's sovereignty. It would be more than 300 years before Canada would proclaim itself a separate nation, and then a further 80-odd years before Newfoundland would join that confederation. But the beginning was here, so it seems most appropriate to begin another nation-spanning adventure here in 1987.

Down from Signal Hill the runners bore the flame the first day to Holyrood on Conception Bay, once a pirate's lair, and, on the next, to Placentia Bay, before crossing by air to Nova Scotia. The flame was carried from Sydney to Halifax and

Andrew Stawicki

16

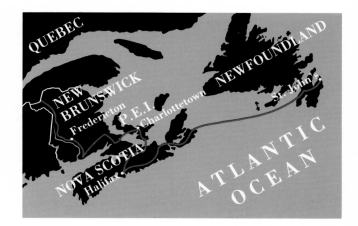

Dartmouth, and up again to Pictou and the ferry to Prince Edward Island, the place the Micmac Indians called "The Cradle in the Waves." On from there again by ferry to New Brunswick and from Saint John, west and north, up the Saint John River Valley, following the path many United Empire Loyalists took in the 1780s.

Gradually, the names of the towns and villages change. Names like King's Landing, Bristol, Bath, and Upper Kent give way to St-André, St-Amand, Bellefleur, St-Léonard, Rivière-Verte. Ahead, through the wooded hills of Madawaska, lies the New Brunswick-Quebec border and, not far beyond, the St. Lawrence, the River of Canada as it has been called, the ancient highway into the centre of the continent.

—*George Bain*

The day before the relay began was blustery and cold, but colourful frame houses brightened the streets of St. John's, Newfoundland, where John McKillop, 60, showed off his dream car, a 1930 Model "A" roadster. Retired as Deputy Minister of Mines and Energy for Newfoundland and Labrador, McKillop now trains daily for 26-mile marathons. On November 17, McKillop realized one more dream, when he carried the Olympic torch for Canada on the first day of the relay.

Excitement grew in St. John's, as Newfoundlanders and torchbearers from across Canada gathered the day before the relay.

I—They spend a lot of their time battling and cursing flames at opposite ends of the country, but they celebrated the Olympic flame together in St. John's. Firefighters Charlie Dunne, 28, from Ferryland, a tiny coastal village south of St. John's, and Lee Cheshire, 34, from Calgary, posed with Fire Captain Arthur Baggs and the lads of "D" shift central of the St. John's Fire Department and their 1942 vintage fire truck. The next day, in a moment of symbolic unity, Charlie passed the torch thousands of miles from east to west— from his hand to Lee's.

II—Lawyer Peter Browne, 26, prepares for his turn with the torch in the solitude of the Quidi Vidi Inlet.

III—Torchbearer and fisherman Joe King, centre back, with his family at Bay Bulls.

II   *Al Harvey*

III   *Al Harvey*

On the eve of the relay, wind-tossed clouds create a sunset of powerful beauty over St. John's. In his cosy study (opposite), Ferd Hayward, the first Newfoundlander to represent Canada at the Olympic Games, reminisces about past Olympics, and looks forward to the next day, when he will share the honour of being the first to carry the Olympic torch with Barbara Ann Scott-King. He still has the shoes he wore on his excruciating 50-km race-walk in the 1952 Summer Olympics in Helsinki. "I made the mistake of wearing shoes that were too tight," recalls 76-year-old Hayward. "When it came time for the race, the flesh on the bottom of my right heel had separated from the bone." Against the advice of doctors, Hayward competed. When he drew into the stadium for the final lap, bent double with pain, a standing crowd cheered him to the finish.

Andrew Stawicki

Al Harvey

Eric Hayes

Eric Hayes

Al Harvey

Al Harvey

Newfoundland, Day 1

On November 17 the Olympic flame came to Canada. Ignited by the rays of the sun in Olympia, Greece, it was carried to Canada in three brass miner's lamps aboard a Canadair Challenger. Frank King, OCO'88 Chairman, Bill Pratt, OCO'88 President, and Roger Jackson, Canadian Olympic Association President, brought the flame to Signal Hill, where the cauldron was ignited. As the first snow of winter fell on Canada's most easterly provincial capital, fireworks boomed overhead and cannons blasted a ceremonial salute from the battery nearby. Braving the icy wind and snow to be a part of the opening of the Olympic torch relay were some thousand spectators.

Prime Minister Brian Mulroney was there, along with wife Mila and son Nicolas, Newfoundland Premier Brian Peckford, and the indomitable John Crosbie. John Murphy, the mayor of St. John's, exchanged gifts with the mayor of Calgary, Ralph Klein. Many glowing words were said and then the Olympic cauldron was lit with the flame from Olympia. With the lighting of the first torch the longest Olympic torch relay in history—88 days and 18,000 kilometres—was set in motion.

Sharing the honor of being the first torchbearers were Ferd Hayward and Barbara Ann Scott-King. Hayward, of St. John's, had been an Olympic race-walker, but on this cold November morning, he moved slowly, savoring the moment. Beside him was Barbara Ann Scott-King, the diminutive fireball who captured the hearts and imaginations of the world in 1948, when she leapt and spun her way to a gold medal in figure skating at the Winter Games in

St. Moritz. Today she was uncharacteristically at a loss for words. "Words," she said, beaming, "I cannot find the words!" Ferd Hayward's eyes welled with tears. They would be the first of millions to be moved by the flame.

Below: Despite the freezing temperatures, school bands, groups of schoolchildren, celebrities, such as Gordon Pinsent, and an appreciative crowd gave the flame a warm welcome.

Following pages: The relay winds its way down Signal Hill after the opening ceremonies.

Andrew Stawicki

Al Harvey

Al Harvey

Al Harvey

Al Harvey

Andrew Stawicki

Al Harvey

Al Harvey

Al Harvey

The first of nearly 7,000 torch transfers was a special moment. The face of Maurice Sheppard, 29, glowed with pride and pleasure as he lit his torch from that of Ferd Hayward and Barbara Ann Scott-King. Sheppard, a six-time provincial judo champion from St. John's, added the second link in what would become the longest human chain in Olympic history and an event that would join all of Canada through the Olympic spirit.

Oblivious to the cold, enthusiastic crowds of school children waved tiny Canadian flags—a ritual that would be repeated countless times in cities, towns, and whistle-stops across a vast country.

Andrew Stawicki

Andrew Stawicki

Al Harvey

A lone woman and child enjoy the passing of the relay from the side of a wintry road on the first day. The relay cavalcade included a media vehicle (opposite), organized by Petro-Canada, which carried a lively and varying group of people bearing cameras with the logos of CBC, CTV, NBC, ABC, and CBS, as well as many independent networks.

Andrew Stawicki

I *Eric Hayes*

II *Eric Hayes*

IV *Eric Hayes*

II *Andrew Stawicki*

I—Sub-Lieutenant Simon Hughes salutes smartly from the quarterdeck of HMCS *Athabaskan* in Halifax Harbour. The following day he exchanged his uniform for the red and white track suit of a torchbearer.

II—Mining is an important industry in Nova Scotia, and in Cape Breton coal has been mined for three centuries. As the torch relay wound its way through the province, work went on as usual underground. Half an hour after everyone else has left the Phelan Mine, Wayne Butts, 37, of Glace Bay, relaxes after another long day in the dark.

Following pages:

I—Torchbearer Herb Martell, an RCMP officer for 12 years, confers with fellow officer Ron Reid.

II—Arnold MacLean carried the torch on Day 4. Here he poses with the raw material for the Stora Forest Industries pulp and paper plant, proudly displaying the gold watch he received last year for his 25 years of service there.

1   *Andrew Stawicki*

I—Torchbearer Garth Haverstock, 12, is a hockey fan and active in public affairs—he is an honorary member of the Strait Pirate Hockey Club, the Honorary Junior Fire Chief of the Port Hawkesbury Volunteer Fire Department, and campaign assistant for Nova Scotia's fund drive for muscular dystrophy this year.

II—A grin lights the face of Mary Davidson, R.N., mother of four, and an ardent runner.

III—Teacher Gerald Mason shares the torch with his nephew Andrew MacDonald.

II   *Al Harvey*

III   *Andrew Stawicki*

1   Andrew Stawicki

II *Michael Creagan*

The magic of the relay attracted many members of the younger generation, and their enthusiasm and youthful energy were key components of the success of the relay.

I—Zenova Halls exercises her 7-year-old mare, Sue, near Dartmouth. In the last two years, Sue has cost Zenova about $3000 per year, and 14-year-old Zenova has earned every penny of it herself. "I've two very large paper routes," Zenova states matter-of-factly. "That's how I do it." Every day she rises at 4:30 to deliver the *Halifax Chronicle-Herald* to over 100 households before school; at noon she distributes another 50 copies of the *Halifax Mail-Star*. After school, she goes straight to the stable and on weekends, she practically lives there. Zenova's goal is to turn Sue into a show horse, and she's already showing promise. But Sue is also Zenova's greatest companion and closest friend. The only time Zenova doesn't go out to the stable is "when the road is closed." She adds, "I would have loved to carry the torch on horseback, but I don't think they would have appreciated trying to get her in the van."

II—Twelve-year-old Martin Barclay-Simpson paddles a kayak on Lake Banook, Dartmouth, the day before his run with the torch. A member of the Senobe Aquatic Club, his hobbies also include running and model making. Martin has won two gold medals and 27 ribbons in competitions.

Prince Edward Island, Day 9

I *Albert Normandin*

As a new day dawned, the Olympic flame began its tour of Prince Edward Island, a province known for its white sand beaches, red soil and pastoral beauty. Not surprisingly, agriculture, fishing and tourism dominate the economy. From the ferry terminal at Wood Island, the relay travelled to ceremonies at the provincial capital, Charlottetown, then onward to Borden, through numerous community celebrations. In this smallest Canadian province, the flame was welcomed with true Maritime warmth.

I—Torchbearer David Beaton, a self-confessed entrepreneur, pictured at his roller rink, Skate Country.

II—Looking angelic with their candles, about 30 members of the Confederation Centre Boys Choir practice Christmas carols in their schoolroom across from the legislature buildings in Charlottetown. In the front row are torchbearers Alex and Jonathan Godfrey, aged 13 and 9, who both had a turn with the torch on Day 9.

III—Dawn over Northumberland Strait, between Nova Scotia and Prince Edward Island.

II *Albert Normandin*

III *Albert Normandin*

1 *Albert Normandin*

II   *Albert Normandin*

III   *Albert Nordmandin*

I—Torchbearer Cynthia Chugg, 28, enjoys a quiet stroll by the ocean with her husband, Brad, an RCMP officer, and their two children, Ammiel and Phillip. II—Torchbearer and lobster fisherman Bill Johnston with friends Don King, Kevin Ross and George Sorrey. III—P.E.I. is affectionately known as Spud Island, and with good reason. The potatoes cropped from the Island's mineral-rich soil represent a $100 million per year industry to the province. "It's the biggest business in P.E.I. next to government," says torchbearer Danny Walker (left), who has been a potato farmer for a decade, with his father, Felix, Their relatively small 55-acre operation near St. George's is one of only 50 elite farms that produce potato seed for the 650 growers on P.E.I. He adds, "We live and die by it here."

I   *Albert Normandin*

II   *Albert Normandin*

58

I,III—Sheep farmer Richard Davies, 43, and his 14-year-old son, Bradley, with Tory. The Olympic torch relay linked Canadians coast to coast, but it was always a special joy when family members passed the torch from one to another. On Day 9 of the relay, father and son shared that pleasure, when Bradley handed the torch to Richard. II—This farmhouse near Primrose typifies the beauty of this agricultural province.

III *Al Harvey*

I *Al Harvey*

II *Al Harvey*

60

III *Al Harvey*

I,II—Escort runners played an important role in the relay. About 150 escorts, selected from amongst Petro-Canada employees, accompanied the relay on 8-day shifts, in groups of six to twelve. Each public torchbearer was assigned an escort, who would run with the torchbearer and assist wherever necessary. As they usually ran about 15 km a day, the escorts had to fulfil fitness requirements, but they also had to have considerable interpersonal skills. Meeting the public and answering the questions of spectators were also part of an escort runner's day. Most importantly, the escorts were prepared for any emergency that might arise. At all times they carried a thermal blanket and a fire extinguisher.

III—At the evening ceremonies before the flame left Prince Edward Island, people gathered together to support the ideals embodied in the relay. All along the route, the torch inspired this spirit of celebration. For a great many people, this event was a singular moment in their lives, a time that will live on in stories repeated to children and grandchildren over the generations.

New Brunswick, Day 10

Like Nova Scotia and Prince Edward Island, New Brunswick's roots are strongly Scottish and British. United Empire Loyalists spilled over into the western colony from Nova Scotia, adding another flavor to the mixture. But New Brunswick also has a strong French component, and the province is officially bilingual. Acadians expelled from what is now Nova Scotia moved west, many settling in New Brunswick.

Torchbearer Michael Robertson (left) celebrates his Scottish heritage near Saint John, New Brunswick.

Following page:

I—Torchbearer Mark Culberson, 14, his father, Lloyd, 44, his father, Everett, 63, and his father, Carl, 87, represent four of the generations that have lived on this land since 1820, when their ancestors came here from Ireland. But the Culbersons have given up the economic battle to keep the land in the family, and have sold everything but the homestead. Their story is the same as that of thousands of farmers coast to coast who have turned in their tractors and packed up their dreams. Still, they are not bitter. Like so many Canadians they have gone on to other things—Carl to retirement and Lloyd and Everett to a successful heating business.

II—Torchbearer Byron Meredith, 47, wearing the gas mask he's only donned half

I *Albert Normandin*

II *Albert Normandin*

64

a dozen times in the 18 years he has worked at the St. Anne-Nackawic pulp plant. Meredith, who is manager of utilities, maintenance and engineering, thrives on the constant stimulation, the change and the challenge of working daily in an industry which is one of the mainstays of Canada's economy.

III—Dr. Munro Bourne, 77, poses good-naturedly by his backyard pool with his wife of 44 years, Margaret. A three-time Olympian, he captured a bronze medal as a member of Canada's 4x200M relay swim team in 1928,

and is one of the oldest Olympians to carry the torch. Dr. Bourne was a physician for 37 years after he retired from swimming following three successive Olympics— 1928, 1932 and 1936—and is the former physician-in-chief at Reddy Memorial Hospital in Montreal.

Following pages:

Scott Hare, 22, loosens up for his leg of the relay in "The Green," one of Fredericton's most beautiful and historic areas. For many athletes like Scott, the opportunity to carry the Olympic torch was a special thrill.

III   *Al Harvey*

Albert Normandin

I   *Albert Normandin*

II   *James Wilson*

III   *Al Harvey*

IV   *Albert Normandin*

I—Torchbearers Austin Tingley, Max McNicol and Guy Leblanc are all guards at Dorchester Penitentiary.

II—Major Terence Monnon poses in front of an indoor miniature range used to train tank gunners at CFB Gagetown, near Oromocto.

III—Paul Von Richter, 47, (far left) is the "tail-twister" in his local chapter of the Lions Club. His job is to keep things light and right in the Lions den. "I can do anything I want in the club," he says, grinning from ear to ear. "I can rib someone, or just levy a fine." The Lions Clubs across Canada played a vital role in the relay, contacting all torchbearers several times to confirm the date and time of their run, helping with crowds, and selling candles to raise money for charity.

IV—Torchbearer Robert Lang, a physical education student at Saint-Louis-Maillet College in Edmundston, where he plays centre for the university hockey team, is a 10-year veteran of the ice.

I—The Meldrum family of Sackville had a record eight members running in the relay. Wendell Meldrum is a former provincial Attorney-General, Minister of Education and now a judge. His two sons, Kirk and Wynn are partners in a local law firm. On the night before the relay, Wendell and Dorothy Meldrum hosted their sons and their families, who passed the torch from one to another on the tenth day of the relay. From front clockwise: Dorothy, Kirk, Mark, Sarah, Mona, Wendell, Sharon, Allyson, Wynn, Wendy.

II,III—The relay proceeds through a blanket of fresh-fallen snow. And while runners do their kilometres, bundled against the cold, some spectators admire the show from the warmth of indoors.

Following page: The core vehicles of the relay caval-cade wind their way through New Brunswick. Consisting of two motor homes (for torchbearers and escorts, and for relay staff), a lead car carrying two miner's lamps, a media vehicle, and a shuttle van, the caravan was escorted at front and rear by a police cruiser.

I   Albert Normandin

II   Albert Normandin

Al Harvey

When little Bruno Levesque, 4, took the torch he brightened up the day for everyone. The longer he ran, the larger the crowd became, as droves of schoolchildren turned out to cheer on the relay's youngest and smallest torchbearer. In no time at all he was surrounded by a moving, cheering mass of cameras, candles and kids. Finally he decided he'd had enough of the celebrity stuff, so he got a hug from his dad, Gerry, who carried the flame the rest of the way. "That was fun," the three-and-a-half-foot-high sprinter said later. Everyone had to agree.

Tibor Bognar

72

Al Harvey

Al Harvey

FROM HAND TO HAND
Quebec, Day 15—29

P roud Quebecers were on hand to witness Olympic medallist Sylvie Bernier run the first kilometre in La Belle Province. Bernier, 23, who captured a gold medal for diving in 1984, was cheered on by a group of fans that included federal cabinet ministers, Monique Vézina and Bernard Valcourt. As well as running with the torch, Bernier volunteered much of her time to the relay, where her high spirits, charm and vitality were much in evidence. She was the Master of Ceremonies in the Province of Quebec, and she was co-Master of Ceremonies in St. John's and Ottawa. On Day 23, December 9, she made a quick cross-Canada trip to Calgary, where she added to her long list of awards and honours, when she was inducted into the Sports Hall of Fame. Within hours she was back to her relay duties.

Another of Quebec's famous natives, Phil Latulippe (below), shares a moment of the relay with spectators along the route. Well-known for his work with fitness, he is a member of the Order of St. John, the Order of Military Merit and the Order of Canada.

Albert Normandin

I—Phil Latulippe, 68, has run an astounding 160,000 km since the age of 48, when he was "smoking three packs a day, weighed 190 pounds and drinking a lot of beer." Today a trim 135 pounds, he teaches classes and dedicates his fitness projects to raising money for charitable groups. Latulippe, who ran across Canada in 1981, plans yet another cross-country odyssey to raise money in 1989.

II—Evening light silhouettes a church spire at Berthier-sur-Mer.

Following pages:
The full moon rises near Berthier-sur-Mer.

II   *Tibor Bognar*

Tibor Bognar

I—Torchbearer Denise Turcotte, 39, is representative of the many Canadians who are not athletes, but who enjoy a lifestyle that includes sports and the outdoors. A high-school teacher, Denise runs, lifts weights, cross-country skis and takes bicycle trips in the summer.

II—Jean-Louis Lavoie, captured with his dog Manouk as they bring in the firewood at Saint-Honoré, just a few kilometres from the relay route.

III—Germain Bélanger, 26, and Hervé Dubé, 45, of Saint-Jean-Port-Joli, at Bombardier's huge railcar manufacturing plant in La Pocatière, where Bélanger is a painter and Dubé a section head. The cars produced here are destined for railways and subways across North America. Bélanger and Dubé both carried the torch on Day 17.

IV—Torchbearer Sylvain Tremblay works the night shift at Atelier Grani-Marbre, where he cuts and polishes huge slabs of stone weighing up to 800 pounds.

I *Albert Normandin*

II   *Tibor Bognar*

III   *Albert Normandin*

IV   *Albert Normandin*

Tibor Bognar

In the beautiful city of Québec, the influence of 17th century Europe can be seen most clearly, especially inside the walls of the old city. Narrow, cobbled streets are lined with 300-year-old buildings, which have been converted to shops, restaurants and galleries. In this setting the venerable Château Frontenac—constructed in 1893—is a newcomer.

Albert Normandin

I *Albert Normandin*

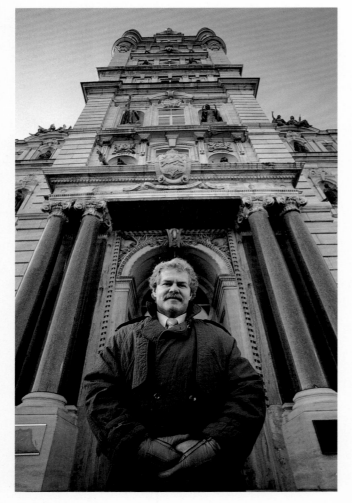

II *Albert Normandin*

III *Michel Gravel*

IV *Michel Gravel*

I—Jean-Louis St-Amand at the Québec Detention Centre, where he counsels through a special outside services program. For this father of six, running with the torch connected him not just to Canada, but to the whole world.

II—"All jobs are dangerous," claims student Richard Grenier, 37, but his part-time job could actually endanger his life. Grenier finances his education by working as a bodyguard for cabinet ministers at the Québec legislature, where he spends much of his time "acting as chauffeur and ensuring the ministers get from appointment to appointment on time."

III—Yvon Vallée, a Québec City bus driver for 16 years, returned to welcoming passengers aboard, after his kilometre with the torch on Day 18.

IV—Physician Sylvie Delisle had an eventful day on December 5. At 8:30 in the morning she carried the Olympic torch near Deschambault; by 2:30 she was at the large, traditional wedding of her brother André and his bride Nathalie, in Pont-Rouge.

I—Torchbearer Margaret Badger and her husband Don, at work on the 100-hectare family farm in the rolling countryside near Knowlton, east of Montréal. The third generation to live on this land, they raise Jersey cows and a herd of 60 Highland cattle. Margaret first started raising Highland cattle because they are easy to care for, but now says, "Once you've had them a little while you fall in love with them."

II—Maurice Lefebvre, 67, is actively involved in the birdwatching club of Sorel. His kilometre with the torch became a big family celebration, as eleven grandchildren and five of his six children turned out.

III—Johanne Brus, with husband Charles, sons Richard and David, and the new calf, "Olympic," named for Johanne's turn with the torch on the day it was born. The Brus's 120-hectare farm supports 130 head of prize-winning Holstein cattle, but Johanne, a farmer all her life, still finds time to run competitively almost every weekend. She was nicknamed "Iron Woman" for competing in more than one race in a day.

1 *Tibor Bognar*

II   *Albert Normandin*

III   *Albert Normandin*

I—A relay spectator at St. Luke's Anglican Church in Waterloo, Québec.

II—The fastest wheelchair marathon athlete in the world, André Viger, carried the torch on Day 23 through his home town of Sherbrooke. Viger, 35, has been a paraplegic since an auto accident at the age of 20. Since that terrible day when his friend fell asleep at the wheel, Viger has taken control of his life and charged after his goals— winning countless international marathons, including three Boston Marathons. His success stems from a fierce determination to live fully. "I don't want to survive," said Viger. "I want to be alive. Yesterday is over and today is all I have."

III—Alwyn Morris, 1984 Olympic gold medallist in kayaking, bore the torch through his home reserve, Kahnawake. The feeling was one of jubilation as Morris ran through the spectators. Cheered on by over 750 Mohawks, an exuberant Morris said, "I couldn't be happier!"

II   *Tibor Bognar*

III   *Michel Gravel*

1   *Albert Normandin*

I,II,III—The relay crosses the bridge in Pierreville (below left) on the morning of Day 21. This area of Québec is characterized by charming villages and 19th century farms—typically long, narrow strips of land fronting on the river. In Québec, the many beautiful churches throughout the province, such as Saint-Joachim, at Châteauguay (below), provided spectacular sites for ceremonies and salutes as the torch passed through.

II   *Albert Normandin*

III   *Michel Gravel*

I *Michel Gravel*

II *Albert Normandin*

III *Tibor Bognar*

I—Wayside crosses occur frequently throughout the countryside in Québec, and range from simple wooden crosses with a ladder and spear, to elaborate crucifixes with statues, such as this one near Pont-Rouge.

II—Normand Aubin, former Toronto Maple Leafs centreman, taking a break from the action at the afternoon game between his hometown team, the Sorel Blues, and a team from Chomedey. Aubin is now a foreman at Soreltex, a carpet factory in Sorel, but he's still active in the game he loves. That same evening he ran with the torch on Day 20 of the relay.

III—Canada's second largest city, Montréal, on the eve of the relay.

Like an adolescent torn between pride and jealousy, Montréal prepared to lose its status of only child in the Canadian family of cities hosting the Olympic Games.

When the flame returned in mid-December, it reminded Montréal that a city in the west, the oil town of Calgary, would soon also play host to athletes from around the world. And although controversy still surrounds the cost of Montréal's role as host of the 1976 Summer Olympics, when the 1987 torch circled the stadium, the magic of the ancient ritual asserted itself again. Even smokers, who contribute two or three cents to the Olympic debt kitty with every cigarette, were appeased.

Two hours earlier, at the corner of Peel and Sainte-Catherine, the fierce wrestler, Mad Dog Vachon, had wept like a baby as he grasped the torch. "I feel emotion in my whole body," he said, innocent as a child from his wheelchair perch. And indeed, to commune with the mystique of this flame, one must become a child again, wide-eyed and innocent.

When the flame arrived at city hall, especially when the cauldron at the main entrance was lit, something happened. This flame has a way of sending shivers up the spine; of awakening old dreams of brotherhood; of reminding us that the Olympics celebrated excellence long before it became the current buzzword; of testifying that the rally revived by the Baron de Coubertin is still the most popular in the world. In a word, the flame awakens the kind of euphoria that washed over Montréal for two weeks one summer and that would soon warm hearts in Calgary. "Lucky people," nostalgic Montrealers seemed to say, not without a trace of jealousy. "Enjoy it!"

—*Gérald Leblanc*

Colin Price

94

Michel Gravel

I   *Arne Glassbourg*

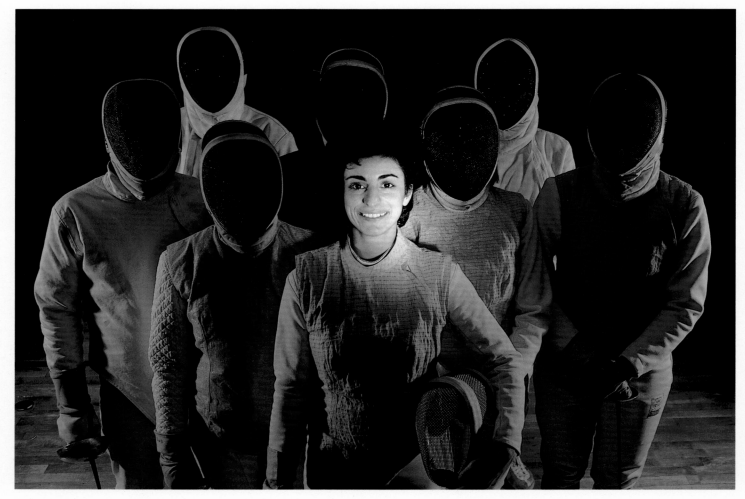

II   *Arne Glassbourg*

III *Stephen Homer*

IV *Stephen Homer*

I—Student Sabine Di Filippo, 20 years old and an international-level water polo player, at Montreal's historic Palestre Nationale pool, built in 1919. Compared to the toughness of Di Filippo's sport—testified by her black eye—her turn with the torch was a relaxing jaunt.

II—Torchbearer Silva Sarkissian, member of the 1986 Canadian championship fencing team, poses with the members of the Bois-de-Boulogne Fencing Club. A student at the University of Montréal, she also works on the monthly publication of the Armenian community, *Nor Ayk*.

III—At the Québec Deli Restaurant, at the corner of Saint-Gérard and Jarry streets in Montréal, waitress of 21 years, Amélie Doucet, is shown the appreciation of her co-workers. Doucet, 35, has worked here for 12 years, and the staff and customers of this cafe are now like family to her. She carried the torch on Day 27.

IV—Concertmaster and torchbearer Suzanne Guimont, in concert with the Orchestra CMAC.

The business community (including some of its future members) was well represented in Québec.

I—Scott Abelson, 16, with some of his classmates on the grounds of Sedbergh Private Boys School, established about 50 years ago to educate Canada's future business elite. Scott was inspired to be a torchbearer by witnessing the excitement generated by the 1984 torch relay in the United States.

II—At the Windsor Hotel in Montréal, torchbearer Paul Enros (right), poses with international business-man Charles Bronfman. Enros is the summer coordinator for the Charles R. Bronfman Youth Educational Organization, a nonprofit organization providing youth with a cultural experience through a sports exchange program.

III—True company and Olympic spirit were exhibited by the employees of Leopold Property Consultants, who applied en masse to be torchbearers. Here nine of the ten employees that ran with the torch on Day 16 pose with President Stephen Leopold.

1 *Stephen Homer*

INTO THE HEARTLAND
Ontario, Day 30—51

Ontario is a province of contrasts. Its population of over 9 million makes it Canada's most populous province, yet nine-tenths of Ontario is a vast wilderness with only sparse human settlement. It is the centre for Canadian manufacturing and business, but large tracts of land are set aside for parks and wilderness areas. And while the first settlers were of predominantly British origin, today's Ontarians are a rich mixture of many different cultures.

The relay entered Ontario at Ottawa—a most fitting place to begin. Here in the nation's capital several thousand people packed together at the Peace Tower to await the arrival of the torch. Winter was in fine form when Ontario welcomed the Olympic torch relay. Big flakes drifted from a thick, woolly sky and all along Wellington Street in downtown Ottawa, the flags were stirred by a light west wind. It seemed to underline the fact that this event was setting records in many ways—including being the coldest torch relay in history, if the Canadian winter was true to form.

Anna Beaudry

Stephen Homer

At 9 a.m. the relay crossed the bridge spanning the Ottawa River, bringing the torch from Hull, Québec to Ottawa. The second runner in Ontario, 16-year-old Kristi Lambert, carried the torch to Parliament Hill, where Prime Minister Brian Mulroney, Liberal leader John Turner, New Democratic leader Ed Broadbent, and other dignitaries waited. At the ceremony, the minister of state for fitness and amateur sport, Otto Jelinek, said, "What a proud day for Kristi, for all of us here at the House of Commons and for all Canadians." Prime Minister Mulroney spoke for many when he said, "We have witnessed touching, moving moments along the relay and been reminded that this is a country of small towns and big dreams."

From the ceremony on Parliament Hill, the relay wound through Ottawa to the city hall, where it was greeted with more crowds, giving the torch a warm send-off on the next leg of its cross-Canada journey.
Following pages:
Torchbearer and moto-cross racer Robert Solmes demonstrates his prize-winning form at a snow-covered site near Foxboro. Solmes, 27, has been racing the bikes since he was 19, competing in events all across Canada, and is currently tenth in Canada in the 500 cc outdoor moto-cross class. Solmes's hobby is all-consuming; he spends all of his spare time and most of his cash on bikes, parts, gas and travel from April to October. And while the airborne gymnastics of the sport may look dangerous to outsiders, Solmes says that his only fear is "not being able to do it the next year."

Stephen Homer

Anna Beaudry

Colin Price

I *Colin Price*

II *Anna Beaudry*

108

III   *Stephen Homer*

IV   *Stephen Homer*

Torchbearers were picked by lottery and the laws of chance revealed a wide cross-section of Canadians at work.

I—Eugenie Wolsey and her husband raise thoroughbred horses on their land near Cannington, west of Peterborough.

II—Cathy Scott, 25, graduated as a drilling and blasting technician, and now works as a construction inspector. During the off-season for construction, she operates a snowplow in Manotick.

III—Bruce Patterson on the road for Atlantic Packaging Products, where he has been a truck driver for 16 years. A few years ago Patterson, 45, put away the cigarettes and picked up the cross-country skis and running shoes. Three times a week he makes a 16-hour run, but now when his truck is parked at the end of his run, you'll find him, not curled up in his cab or in the nearest roadside cafe, but out jogging.

IV—Joe Maxine, from Peterborough, evidently enjoying his break from the roofing trade.

Marthe Love

Stephen Homer

Stephen Homer

Marthe Love

Stephen Homer

Stephen Homer

Stephen Homer

Cornwall, Bonville, Ingleside, Lyn, Kingston, Salem, Deseronto, Omemee, Peterborough, Port Hope, Pickering, Locust Hill, Newmarket—in small towns and large centres, at ceremonies and salutes and at roadsides, people took time out of their lives to greet the torch. They put on their medals and their best clothes and they promenaded their fancy haircuts. They came out in rain and snow, sheltering under brightly coloured umbrellas. They brought their children and their pets and if they didn't all carry the Olympic torch, many carried Olympic candles or their own homemade versions of the torch. The flame became a rallying point for Canadians, who displayed the national flag with renewed vigour—some hoisting it in unorthodox ways. Everywhere, people crowded around to touch the torch and to take a little bit of the fire with them.

Following pages:

The countryside northeast of Port Hope.

John De Visser

Colin Price

George Gooderham

Heading south through Ontario, the highway stretched like an endless ribbon in front of the caravan, beckoning it onward to Calgary. In Ontario's densely populated southern section, the stops became more frequent and the crowds larger. At each stop the reception—warm, enthusiastic and heartfelt—added to the ever-increasing excitement as the relay neared Toronto.

Following pages:
Toronto's celebration at Nathan Phillips Square,

on the eve of the relay, had set the stage for the biggest outpouring of enthusiasm to date on the cross-Canada adventure. The next morning there was a heightened sense of expectation as the relay caravan entered Canada's largest city. From the starting point at the corner of Highway 7 and Yonge Street to the heart of downtown—some 22 kilometres—people streamed out by the thousands to watch the relay pass. They crawled onto roofs, hung out of windows, and even scaled statues and stood on telephone booths.

George Gooderham

Boris Spremo

At 12:34 p.m. Olympic medallist Ben Johnson stepped from the sidewalk to carry the torch the last kilometre into Nathan Phillips Square. Johnson, who had shattered the world 100-metre dash record just three months ago, worked his way through a dense crowd. When he entered the square and mounted the stage, a deafening cheer rose from a crowd of thousands.

George Gooderham

Boris Spremo

David Sedman

Canada's fastest woman sprinter, Angella Issajenko, took the torch from the world's fastest man, Ben Johnson, at the Toronto ceremony. With a spring in her step she carried the torch out of the square, smiling broadly at the crowds lining the streets. Issajenko, 29, helped her team to an Olympic silver medal in the 4x100M relay in 1984.

Ottmar Bierwagen

I   *Stephen Homer*

II   *John Reeves*

To most torchbearers the relay was a high point in their lives and after the excitement, they returned to their daily routines. But looking behind the scenes, it became clear that the average Canadian leads no ordinary life.

I—Ed Clifford, assistant editor at Toronto's *Globe and Mail,* is used to the hectic pace of the newsroom, and his leisure time is also filled with many activities, from drag racing to running. He writes, "In 1986, I did win a gold medal in a 3-kilometre road race—for being the oldest runner! What the heck, at 54 you take all the gold medals you can get; no questions asked."

II—Tiffany Bridges gets into a festive holiday mood at Tuxedo, a salon in Toronto's fashionable Yorkville district. A former Miss Teen Richmond Hill, she has a degree in English literature, and plans to travel the world.

III—Gary Mitchell, Peter Dopping and Murray Lively at the General Motors plant in Oshawa, where they all work.

IV—Stephen Moysey is a corporate travel consultant, but more than that, he is a squash champion and one of the sport's biggest fans. As part of Canada's inaugural team at the world squash championships in 1970, he won his match against India. Later he helped develop Canada's first commercial squash complex, located in Toronto.

V—Principal Jim Grieve with his students at Windfields Junior High in North York. Grieve's students were thrilled for him, but not as thrilled as Grieve, who is a self-confessed nationalist and who was very proud to carry the torch.

V   *Stephen Homer*

III *Stephen Homer*

IV *Edward Gajdel*

Christmas can be very grand in Toronto. Just follow the miles of sparkling white lights along University Avenue, the broad avenue extending from Bloor Street, the city's staggeringly expensive shopping district with its huge tinsel-gold trees. It will take you down around Queen's Park, the sober, pink stone palace housing Ontario's parliament. Follow University Avenue past the gaily decorated Hospital for Sick Children to the banks and brokerages and law firms downtown. The dazzle is grand indeed.

Of course, in Toronto the surest signs of Christmas are probably the office lunches which fill even the dowdiest restaurants with merry workers who all go back to work late, riotously unapologetic, and who all leave early. This huge city with a metropolitan population of nearly 2.1 million loves Christmas.

This year, however, Christmas spirit was late coming to Toronto. Maybe it was because of the mild December

I   *Perry Zavitz*

II   *Jim Elzinga*

V   *Stephen Homer*

126

III *Dawn Goss*

IV *Peter Sibbald*

weather; we do like a little snow, thank you. But the feeling changed on December 23, when more than 40,000 people came out to see the torch carried into the city.

Toronto's own Ben Johnson carried the torch into Nathan Phillips Square at City Hall. Johnson was one of 34 runners who carried the torch through the city—holding up the traffic, throwing the daily hurly burly of Chinatown along Dundas Street into an even noisier uproar, clogging the bumper-to-bumper chaos of Yonge Street. No one, not even the permanently grouchy cabbies, complained. For the first time, people looked at each other and said, "You know, it feels like Christmas."   —*Stevie Cameron*

Torchbearers celebrated the Christmas season in their own styles and traditions.
I—Keith Kinniburgh with the Christmas bird, surrounded by his wife (left), and her family.
II—Sheila Christmas sets the mood for her Christmas table with Olympic torch candles. Her torch run on Christmas Eve almost eclipsed seasonal festivities. "Christmas comes every year," she said. "But the torch only comes once."
III—Debra Anne King, 10, and her cat Millie dream amongst the Christmas presents. Debra worked hard, running with a hammer for weight, to get into shape for her run.
IV—Frank Halcro enjoys a traditional meal within his warm family circle.
V—Strings of brightly coloured bulbs light the dark winter night with the warmth of Christmas.

II *David Sedman*

III *Grant Black*

I—Eight-year-old David Visschedyk cuddles a favourite Christmas present, his new kitten named Bullet. David has successfully completed chemotherapy treatments for a type of bone cancer. His active, busy life includes playing street hockey with his friends almost daily. David's torchbearer track suit is one of his most treasured possessions and he wears it everywhere, complete with all the buttons he got on the relay.

II—Otto Jelinek, the minister of state for fitness and amateur sport, carried the torch with his sister Maria through Oakville on Christmas Eve. The brother and sister team were the world pairs figure skating champions in 1962.

III—Susan Thibert was especially thrilled at running with the Olympic torch. Thibert, 24, has won many ribbons at the Special Olympics, her most outstanding achievement being a silver medal in swimming. Her involvement with the Special Olympics, and the sense of fulfilment she obtained, motivated her to be a torchbearer.

A torchbearer mosaic—motorcycles, medicine, medals and metal.

I—Near Sarnia Harbour John and Maryann Edgar pose with fellow members of the Vintage Motorcycle Club, established to preserve and restore old motorcycles.

II—James Forrest with his surgeon's tools at Leamington District Memorial Hospital.

III—Leslie MacDonald, 81, with the diploma and the bronze medal he won as coxswain of the Canadian Olympic stroking eight at the 1932 Games.

IV—Steve Szabo, 52, is a machine operator for Atlas Specialty Steels in Welland.

Following pages:

The relay passes through the area around Port Alma.

II   *David Sedman*

III   *Peter Sibbald*

IV   *Jim Elzinga*

Marthe Love

People used words like proud, joyful, and honoured to describe their feelings when they carried the torch. Many were moved to tears. Everyone, young and old, became caught up in the moment.

I—Bill Hewson shares a big hug with his son David, 5.

II—Raymond Bauer, hockey Olympian and brother of Father David Bauer, one of Canada's hockey pioneers, enjoys a special moment with David Hollingworth, 11.

III—Carl Hiebert's happiness is contagious as he gives a "thumbs-up" salute to the crowd in Stratford.

Hiebert flew his ultralight plane from Halifax to Vancouver for Expo 86, raising $90,000 for the Canadian Paraplegic Association.

IV—The new year is symbolic of new beginnings and new hope. On New Year's Day, Larry O'Connor ran with the torch, perhaps remembering his own past dreams and considerable triumphs and thinking of future hopes. O'Connor, 76, who was a member of the Canadian Olympic track and field team in 1936, ran with an implanted heart pacemaker.

I   *Greg Stott*

II   *Greg Stott*

III *Greg Stott*

IV   *Grant Black*

134

7:30 a.m. Brian gets his torchbearer track suit.

Torchbearer Brian MacLean, 33, of London, Ontario, was born in England and moved to Canada when he was five. On January 3, he rose at 5:00 a.m., in order to be at the torchbearer assembly point, the Lions Club Hall in Strathroy, by 7:30.

After donning their track suits, the group, ten in all, gathered for the briefing session, led by a trio of escort runners called "The Three Amigos," and two shuttle van drivers, "The Odd Couple." They quickly covered the history of the Games, the torch and the relay, and then asked the runners to introduce themselves and let everyone know how many applications they had filled out. Unlike most, Brian had filled out just five.

Next came the most important part of the briefing—safety. "The toques should be worn at all times," said Hugh Ahearn. "When some people get their hands around the torch, they forget quickly that fire burns—especially hair." When one bald torchbearer quipped, "I've got no problem," Brian came back quickly with, "That's what happens when you don't wear a toque." The place roared with laughter, setting the tone for the friendly spirit of camaraderie that would envelop the group.

The briefing over, they boarded the shuttle van, which would get them to the relay route. At 9:15 a.m. the flashing lights of the lead police car appeared in the distance. By that time the sun was shining brightly and clusters of spectators lined the highway. Then everything began to move quickly. Everyone transferred to "Torch 1," the relay core vehicle for torchbearers. There the excitement really started to build, everyone craning out the windows and through the doors to get a better view. One by one the members of the group—who had named themselves "The Spirit of '88"— took their turns, until finally Brian advanced to the hotseat next to the door. At 10:29 he leapt out, got a hug from his teammate Cindy, and took off over the pavement.

In six minutes it was over, all but the euphoria. "When you get your hand on it, you know it's there," he said. "It got so hot, I had to take my gloves off. It just went through me." But what went through Brian MacLean that sunny Sunday wasn't the heat of the flame. It was that inexplicable feeling that overcame all those in contact with it—the Olympic mystique.

By noon he was on his way home. Like all the others who had gone before him and who would follow after, he had, in the space of six minutes, become a part of Olympic—and Canadian— history.

7:43 a.m. A trio of escort runners and two drivers brief the torchbearers at the Lions Club Hall.

Photos by Grant Black

8:18 a.m. The group heads off to join the relay in their shuttle van, Torch 13.

9:00 a.m. The van arrives at the relay route, soon to rendezvous with Torch 1.

9:25 a.m. Everyone transfers to Torch 1. Brian eagerly awaits his turn.

10:29 a.m. The moment finally arrives, and Brian is off, carrying the torch.

10:31 a.m. A quick stop for pictures with his family and he's off again.

11:30 a.m. "The Spirit of '88" at the debriefing session, back at the Lions Club.

I,III—A crowd estimated at between 10 and 15 thousand lit up the night at the ceremony in London on Day 48. Even the youngest raised Olympic candles in a joyous salute to the torch. People started arriving up to four hours before the scheduled arrival of the relay to enjoy live music, dance and figure skating performances. The huge reception in this city of some 280,000 was representative of the high level of support the relay would see throughout Ontario.

II—For Heather Freer, of Petrolia, the elation of carrying the torch merged with the euphoria of giving birth. Eight hours after Freer ran through the crowded streets of Sarnia, she gave birth to a daughter, Alyssa Marlo. Freer decided to run with the encouragement of her husband, Jay, and her doctor, who both accompanied her on the run. Later, as she lay resting in her hospital bed, she talked about the excitement of both events. "Both carrying the torch and having my baby were about even." But then she added, "Maybe the baby was a bit more important."

I   *Grant Black*

II   *Greg Stott*

III   *Grant Black*

1 Greg Stott

II *Greg Stott*

III *Greg Stott*

IV *Grant Black*

Thousands of people participated directly in the relay and millions more participated as spectators. The spell of the event was far-flung, drawing in Canadians of an amazing diversity. Only a few were left untouched.

I—Though the flame came within a few kilometres of their door, the Bowmans had no knowledge of its passing, or of the Olympic Games. They are a Mennonite family of the "Old Order," a group which adheres staunchly to the old ways of farming, without electricity, heat or running water. While the world rushes on about them, they create for themselves an existence that is much the same as their ancestors' for centuries past.

II—Denyse Provost, at the ceremony at CFB Borden. When the flame came through Camp Borden, it got a rousing welcome from the soldiers stationed there.

III—Betty White bundles up for the relay.

IV—The King family of Guelph took no chances of missing out on this historic event.

The Canadian landscape has an austere beauty in winter. It is a land stilled by cold and even when it is at its most serene, there is the edge of danger that extreme temperatures bring. But far from being intimidated by the cold, Canadians are quick to take advantage of the season—with ice skating, skiing, snowshoeing, snowmobiling, tobogganing and, of course, that all-Canadian pastime: hockey.

I   *Grant Black*

II   *Grant Black*

I—A field near Brantford.

II—A frozen pond near Strathroy. These informal hockey games, played wherever there is a patch of ice, are a familiar sight across Ontario.

III—A lone torchbearer crosses northern Ontario on Day 51. The next day, the snowmobile portion of the relay would begin, as it entered some of the coldest and least populated areas of the cross-country trek.

Grant Black

THE PACE QUICKENS
Ontario, Manitoba, Saskatchewan, Day 52—63

Grant Black

For ten days the Olympic torch relay took to snowmobile for the crossing of 2,800 kilometres of frozen, sometimes desolate terrain. Here in the heart of the continent, winter rules with a firm hand, and relay organizers had taken that into account.

For the portion of the relay from Shanty Bay, Ontario to Prince Albert, Saskatchewan, three Bombardier Safari 503 snowmobiles were provided. They were equipped with wheels as well as skis, protective bars, rear-view mirrors and heated handlebars. At speeds of 30 to 50 kilometres per hour, the relay quickly ate up the kilometres, but planners also ensured that the flame was run into and out of the ceremonies, and that torchbearers had a chance to carry the torch on foot. After each group had taken their motorized tour, members ran together for a kilometre, handing-off the flame from one to another.

Just as the sun crested the horizon at Lake Simcoe, Father Maurice Ouimet (left), boarded the snowmobile for his kilometre with the torch. For many years Father Ouimet had served five parishes in the wilderness west of James Bay. In the 1950s he approached his long-time friend Joseph-Armand Bombardier about creating a motorized vehicle to make his long-distance rounds easier. Bombardier responded with the prototype of today's snowmobile, making Father Ouimet the first Canadian to own a snowmobile.

I—"I saw the flame yesterday. I wanted to blow my horn, but it was too caked with snow," said Francis Pigeon, 29, of Elliott Lake, who had been on the road for 26 hours continuously.

II—Running with the torch was a break from the high stress of David Harris's job as air traffic controller at Thunder Bay Airport.

III—Robert Zufelt good-humouredly relives his moment with the flame at Sault Ste. Marie.

II   *Tom Skudra*

III   *Greg Stott*

1 George Gooderham

II   *Greg Stott*

Canada's finest young athletes came out to carry the torch, bringing to the relay their experiences as competitors as well as their pride as Canadians.

I—When Liisa Savijarvi ran with the torch, it was a personal victory of will. A year earlier she had lost control on a ski run at Vail, Colorado, and ended up in a hospital bed. Coaches said she might never ski again; doctors said she might never walk again. But on Day 52 she ran along with the torch, the first time she had run since her injury.

II—For swimmer Alex Baumann, whose double Olympic golds and double world records in the 400 and 200 individual medleys had stood for three years, carrying the flame had its own impact. "It took me back to '84," he said. "I haven't seen this kind of emotion since then." Baumann's philosophy—that if you hold fast to your dreams and refuse to give up, others will follow you—was borne out by the children who called him by his first name and reached out to him as he cruised by with the torch.

II *Grant Black*

I—Jim Cada, 23, runs into the Blind River salute, wearing traditionally decorated mitts made by his mother. Cada is Ojibway, and is the maintenance manager for the Mississauga Indian band.

II—David Doucette, 15, with the picture of his brother Jason that he carried when he ran in the torch relay on Day 55. Jason was 12 when he tragically drowned on the day his family received the news that he had been chosen as a torchbearer. With the support of his parents, David ran in place of his brother, saying, "I've been looking forward to it. It makes me happy to be able to run for him instead of someone else doing it who didn't even know him." Jason's room, full of trophies and memorabilia, attests to a life of achievement, activity and happiness, an ability to rise to any challenge. When David said, "I'll celebrate his fighting spirit the most," he was paying tribute to his brother's life.

III—At the Terry Fox Memorial at Thunder Bay, the relay paused to honour the one-legged runner who had set an example of courage and conviction for all of Canada. It was here that Terry Fox ended his Marathon of Hope, after raising $24 million for cancer research. The inscription on the base of the statue reads: "He united Canadians as they have never been united before." When the caravan reached the cold, windswept statue there were few words, as the relay cavalcade paid its respects to one of Canada's heroes.

III *Greg Stott*

Manitoba, Day 59

When the torch crossed into Manitoba from Ontario, it was late in the afternoon of Day 59. Within 100 kilometres of the border the landscape had changed from the dense coniferous growth and rock of the Precambrian shield to a flat and open landscape— the fertile prairie for which Manitoba is famed.

By 9:00 p.m. the torch reached the outskirts of Winnipeg. For two centuries Winnipeg was the hub of the entire prairie region, first for the fur trade, and then as an essential railway terminus for the surrounding grain-growing areas. Today the city is a fascinating mixture of historic buildings and innovative architecture.

Gordon Nicholson (opposite), delivers mail along historic Broadway Avenue, a few days before his run with the torch.

Following pages:

I—Manitoba's legislature building, completed in 1919, with its famed Golden Boy, holding aloft a torch. On Day 60, Premier Howard Pawley and other dignitaries gathered here with about 1,000 onlookers to cheer the Olympic torch onto the stage.

II—On Day 59 Jerin Stanlake, 15, carried the torch as well as the newspapers for his route.

Art Turner

Art Turner

III—Torchbearer Laurence de March peers through a tank of young Arctic grayling at the University of Manitoba's freshwater institute, where he is a biologist.

IV—Clifford Pockett displays a fresh batch of Canadian one-dollar coins, known as "loons," at the Royal Canadian Mint in Winnipeg. Pockett, who was a torchbearer on Day 59, has worked at the Mint for 12 years.

Following pages:

As the torch swept across Manitoba on snowmobile, it generated a new kind of excitement, from the convoy of 11 private snowmobiles that escorted the torch into Ste. Anne, to its reception in small towns as it crossed into Saskatchewan.

II *Brian Milne*

III *Art Turner*

IV *Art Turner*

Relais du flambeau olympique

Grant Black

Saskatchewan, Day 61

Brian Milne

Gabriel Franchère, a French-Canadian fur trader who made his way to Lake Winnipeg from Fort Vermilion in the early summer of 1814, was dazzled by what he saw. The diverse harmony of land and sky along the Saskatchewan River, he wrote, "pours contentment and joy into the soul of the enchanted spectator." Why then, he asked himself, do the prairies not overflow with human life?

He found his answer in the winter. Then, he wrote, "Nature has lost all her beauty." Yet those who came after him—the men and women who carved the rolling earth into human proportions and whose own lives in turn were shaped by the land—knew that January and February can bring an extreme beauty to the plains. A beauty of brief days as blue as any ocean, and of long nights illuminated by the distant fire of the stars. A beauty, silent except for the constantly moaning wind, that is the beginning of terror.

Winter reminds us that although we own and use and abuse the land, we never entirely control it. Settlers who braved the harsh conditions had the chance to remake their lives, and the place-names of rural Saskatchewan give proof of their hope: Virgin River, Eldorado, Paradise Hill. When times are hard and hope is deferred, the place-names grow sombre: Snare Lake, Holdfast, Deception Lake. Sometimes all hope is relinquished: Bone Creek, Perdue.

It was through this windbeaten land, through the long miles invisibly stained by the hopes of wheatmen, cattlemen and oilmen, that hundreds of proud westerners carried a maple torch. The torch relay forced a confrontation of elements: fire and ice. And without the entourage of supporters and onlookers, cars, trucks and shuttle vans, you're left with a simple image: a torchbearer dressed in red, treading on a white world.

In this struggle between the elements, fire apparently won. Even in the starkest cold, the runners would not give up and the flame would not go out. But when the torch had disappeared, leaving its ration of contentment and joy in the souls of some enchanted spectators, the ice and snow remained. Unmelted. Implacable. Beautiful.

— *Mark Abley*

Brian Milne

I   *Tom Skudra*

II   *Tom Skudra*

III   *Douglas Walker*

I—Martin and Myrna Luther at their farm, "Riskan Hope," near Craik. Martin, born in 1912, has lived in Craik all his life, a fourth-generation farmer in the area. The couple has two children and five grandchildren. That evening, when the torch passed right by their gate, the Luthers came out with their own torch and some candles to celebrate the flame.

II—Bennett's Garage, in Chamberlain, has been in the Bennett family since 1918, and this building was built in 1944. While Petro-Canada employees were not eligible to be torchbearers, Cleve Bennett and his son Lyle got into the spirit of the relay. When it came through, in the early evening, the Bennetts handed out balloons and flags to the spectators.

III—Colins Geber and Joyce Paquette with Tutor jets at the Moose Jaw Canadian Armed Forces base. Both torchbearers, Geber and Paquette trained together in aviation life support and as troubleshooters for these jets—the same aircraft used by Canada's famous *Snowbirds* aerobatic team.

1   *Tom Skudra*

II *Todd Korol*

I—Torchbearers share a group run near Saskatoon.
II—Jason Headrick, 14, Sea Cadet of the Year for
Saskatchewan in 1986, was a torchbearer on Day 63.
Following pages:
I—Donalda Garner, 39, of Regina, was willing to
relinquish even her precious goats in order to carry
the torch. Garner wanted to run for her father, who
is disabled, and for her kilometre in Quebec, she
sold seven goats in order to raise the fare for herself

I *Douglas Walker*

and her parents. There they stayed at the home of torchbearer Pierre Fafard, receiving "royal" treatment and forging bonds that will endure long after the flame has reached its destination. For Garner it epitomized the true meaning of "share the flame."

II—Torchbearer Gregory Cooper (left), at the RCMP training headquarters for Canada, in Regina. Sergeant Cooper, pictured with Drill Sergeant Ron Williamson, trained here 20 years ago.

III—Grain elevators near Estlin.

II *Douglas Walker*

III   *Douglas Walker*

Gary Fiegehen

Tom Skudra

NORTH BY NORTHWEST
Northwest Territories, Yukon, British Columbia, Day 63—80

On January 18, the flame took to the air for the crossing of Canada's far north, flying from Prince Albert, Saskatchewan, to Yellowknife, the capital and only city in the Northwest Territories. From here the flame would continue its aerial sweep across the roof of the continent, leaving the next day at 11:00 a.m., en route to Inuvik, Canada's largest community north of the Arctic Circle. From Inuvik, it would fly to Whitehorse, capital of the Yukon, and then into British Columbia.

The Northwest Territories occupy more than a third of Canada's area, yet have a population totalling just 52,000. The size and scope of this northern land are virtually incomprehensible to those who have never encountered its vastness. Yet the intrinsic loneliness of the landscape is mediated by the extraordinary warmth of its people.

Here the look of the relay changed, bowing to the necessities of life in the north. It scaled down from about 40 vehicles to 6, and the lead car became a police 4x4 pickup truck—complete with constables clothed, much like the specta-tors, in full-length, fur-rimmed hooded parkas, snow boots and fur-lined flapped hats. In the north, the custom of trav-elling by dogsled is far from extinct, and in Inuvik, the flame was transported in this uniquely north-ern way.

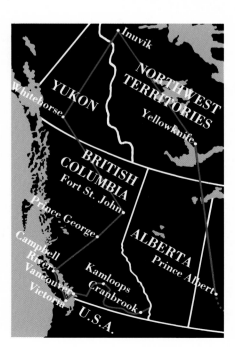

I *Gary Fiegehen*

II *Gary Fiegehen*

I—Mark Eveson, 39, of Yellowknife, works as an open-pit driller at a local gold mine. A single parent, Eveson was delighted that his turn with the torch inspired his son to start training for track and field.

II—Norman Sangris, 15, a Dene who lives in Yellowknife, wears a jacket made by his sister Mary Anne. Norman runs his own trap line, which he accesses by snowmobile, but on weekends he often takes a dog team out.

III—Stan Ruben runs past Our Lady of Victory church in Inuvik. This unique church, designed in the shape of an igloo, was constructed without blueprints, from a drawing. Built in 1958, the church has become a tourist attraction, drawing visitors from as far away as Europe.

IV—Torchbearers Lorraine Lokos, 34, a long-time resident of Inuvik, and Victor Botari, 43, are both actively involved in cross-country skiing in Inuvik. Lokos has skied competitively and Botari teaches the sport.

III *Tom Skudra*

IV *Gary Fiegehen*

169

In Inuvik, the relay logged two firsts: the torch's first foray above the Arctic Circle and the first time it had been transported by dogsled. Torch-bearer Janice Nikkel, from Manitoba, enjoys her ride with the torch on local resident Brian St. Amand's sled.

Tom Skudra

Perry Zavitz

Yukon, Day 64

At 5:30 p.m. the plane carrying the Olympic flame touched down in Whitehorse. Here on the banks of the Yukon, or *Yu-kun-ah*, the "great river" that drains three-quarters of the Yukon, enthusiasm for the torch poured forth. Two out of three Yukoners live in this city of roughly 15,000 residents, and that night many turned out to see the flame.

Yukon is almost synonymous with "gold rush" to many people, but there is a grandeur here that has little to do with the lure of gold. Long before the gold rush of 1890, the Yukon was a land of devastating beauty, of vast mountain ranges and barren expanses of tundra, of the mysterious long night of winter, and of a people uniquely suited to the drama of the north. Today gold still lures many people, but other minerals have taken its place in the economy of the territory.

Snowmobiles have become a practical solution to travel in the north today. But dogsleds, such as torchbearer James Boyde's beautifully constructed sled (left), are still used. Boyde, 44, a biathlete Olympian at Grenoble in 1968, teaches school in Mayo, where he raises and trains dog teams, and skis, canoes and hunts.

I *Perry Zavitz*

II *Perry Zavitz*

III *Perry Zavitz*

IV *Perry Zavitz*

Torchbearers in Whitehorse represented the unique character of the Yukon.

I—Gerry Stockley, 15, lives in Whitehorse, but he lived for nine years in a two-room cabin on Lake Laberge, made famous by poet Robert Service in "The Cremation of Sam McGee." Gerry and his parents stand beside Sam McGee's cabin, now part of a museum.

II—Ron McFadyen, 45, enjoys the Takhini hot springs near Whitehorse. The water in the outdoor springs varies from 35 to 40 degrees Celsius, a startling contrast to the air, which can be minus 30 degrees.

III—Alan Taylor, 24, practises his boxing skills at the native community centre. Taylor represented the Yukon in the Canadian Nationals for three years in a row until 1984. He has remained active in sports and has organized a native men's slowpitch team.

IV—Janet Arntzen, 13, beams out from the fur of her colourful parka at the Anglican log church, built in 1898. Janet was born and raised in the Yukon.

Kharen Hill

I *John Douglas Kenny*

British Columbia, Day 64

The Olympic flame entered British Columbia at close to midnight on Day 64, flying from the white peaks of Whitehorse to the level plains of Fort St. John. Following the ceremony the next morning, it would continue on to Prince George, and then, in a marked change of climate, to Campbell River, on Vancouver Island. In one day the relay would go from temperatures of minus 35 degrees Celsius to a balmy plus 7—from parkas and mitts to windbreakers and, in some cases, even shorts. At Campbell River, the relay team would resume the trek on foot, rejoining the relay vehicles, which had come overland from Prince Albert, Saskatchewan.

Here in Canada's westernmost province, the flame was met with an unabashedly emotional reception, from the cities of the north, to the coast and on into the interior, where the relay encountered some of its most difficult terrain. A province of remarkable diversity, British Columbia is perhaps best known for its mild coastal temperatures, which are moderated by warm ocean currents flowing offshore. As a result, B.C.'s coast is busy year-round with both recreation and industry. Fishing and logging are two major industries, and log booms, such as the one at Courtenay (opposite), are a common sight.

I—Miss Teen Prince George 1987, Roberta Lang, carried the torch in her native city. Roberta, 16, is active in sports, scholastics and community service, and her dream is to participate in the 1992 Olympics.
II—A top-ranked speed skater, Linda Johnson, 16, glided through Fort St. John with the torch.

II *John Douglas Kenny*

I   *Kharen Hill*

II   *Kharen Hill*

I—Hal Ball plays the tuba in the ex-servicemen's Chiefs and Petty Officers Association Band, in Victoria on Day 68.

II— The mystique of the Olympic flame affected both torchbearers and spectators. Everywhere, onlookers wanted to touch the maplewood handle of the torch.

III—At Duncan, the flame is shared with spectators after the ceremony. The sight of people crowding around to light candles from the Olympic flame was a familiar one, but each time the excitement was renewed.

III *Kharen Hill*

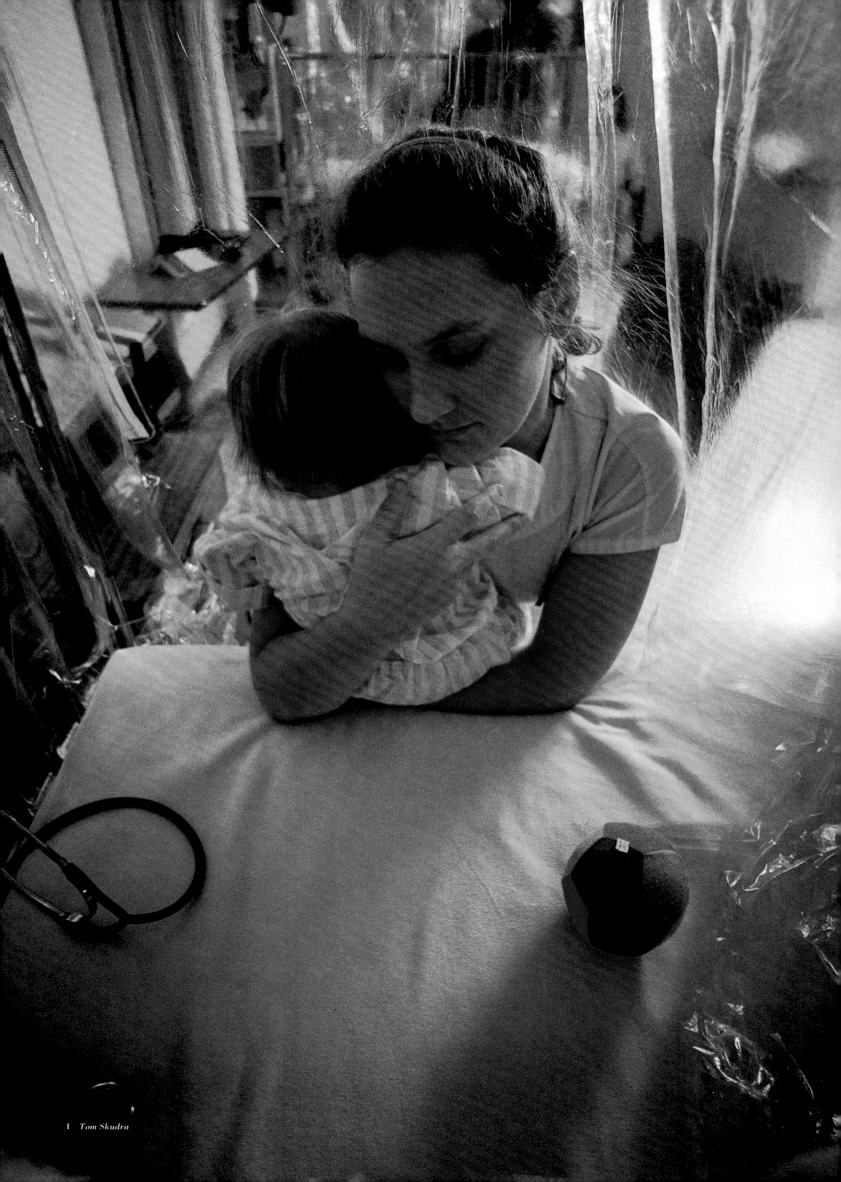

II *Marthe Love*

III *Tom Skudra*

I—Nurse Mary-Louise Stacey gently comforts Kyle Fleming, who is recovering from bronchiolitis at Victoria General Hospital. Stacey, 24, had just returned from her honeymoon when she carried the torch on Day 67.

II—George Harris, 42, lives on the Chemainus Indian Reserve, where he is the business manager for the band. Harris was the centre of congratulations and celebrations, surrounded by friends, relatives and band members, just before he carried the torch in Qualicum on Day 66.

III—Torchbearer Howard Kelsey, a guard with the men's national basketball team for 12 years and now assistant athletic director for the University of Victoria, says, "It's the most dynamic of any sport I've tried. It's got rhythm, quickness, strength, even self-expression." Kelsey (centre) is flanked by Spencer McKay, Cord Clemens, and Geoff McKay. Ken Shields, 42, in the background, coaches the University of Victoria team, which has won the Canadian university title seven of the last eight years.

I   *Tom Skudra*

II   *Kharen Hill*

For three days, the relay was welcomed with
extraordinary enthusiasm in towns and cities
throughout Vancouver Island.

I,II—Tryntje Horn lives with her husband,
musician Paul Horn, on their acreage in Victoria,
in a house she designed herself. Their property,
with an unrestricted view of the ocean, affords
room for her African Nubian goats, a sheep, and
several other dogs and cats. A Dutch-born
Canadian, she came here via the high-fashion
world of Paris, Milan and New York, but her
surroundings today reflect a simpler and more
peaceful life. Tryntje carried a bouquet of tulips
along with the torch on Day 68, in memory of the
Canadian liberators of Holland during the Second
World War. Before her run she trained with her
Rhodesian ridgeback hound, who ran with her in
the relay wearing a special coat that Tryntje had
made for him, decorated with the torch relay
emblem. After she had handed on the torch, she
said with typical enthusiasm, "I went to heaven
without dying. It's going to last me 100 years. It's a
spiritual experience."

III—A group of spectators is silhouetted in
Victoria's Beacon Hill Park, on the relay route.

IV,V—The *Queen of Saanich* carries the flame
through Active Pass in Georgia Strait, en route to
the B.C. mainland on Day 68. On the following
day it would tour Canada's third-largest city,
reaching Canada Place in downtown Vancouver
for a ceremony early in the morning, and taking
the rest of the day to wind through the city and its
outlying areas.

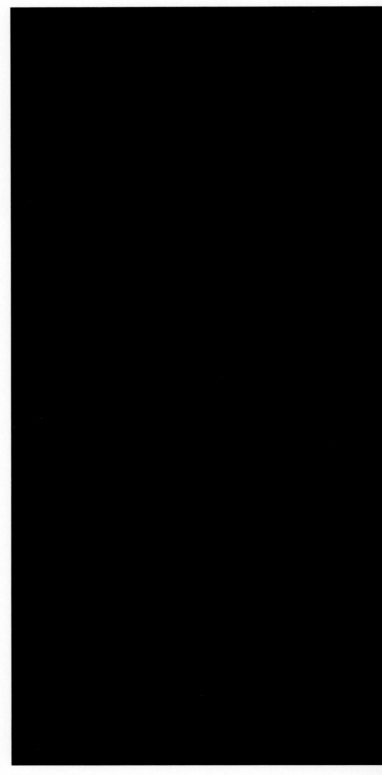

V   *Kharen Hill*

III *Kharen Hill*

IV *Heather Dean*

I *Alan Zenuk*

II *Marthe Love*

III   *Jurgen Vogt*

I—The relay crosses Lions Gate Bridge in Vancouver. II,III—Trevor Woytko, 12, has an emotional moment at the Canada Place ceremony, after handing the torch over to his mentor, Rick Hansen (below). No stranger to public ceremonies, Trevor has participated in the Variety Club's Telethon for the last five years, as well as many other public events—including Hansen's homecoming in 1987 after his Man in Motion World Tour, which raised over $23 million for research and rehabilitation.

In metropolitan Vancouver, with a population of some 1.4 million, torch-bearers reveal a wide variety of work and leisure occupations.

I—Lori Fung trains for an exhausting six and a half hours daily. Fung, 24, is an Olympic gold medallist in rhythmic gymnastics and a six-time Canadian champion in the sport, which uses balls, ribbons, hoops, clubs and ropes. After her run with the torch, an excited Fung said, "It's just a tremendous feeling....Now I know why I come into the gym."

II—Richard Johnson, 24, guides a sailboat past Stanley Park, with the Vancouver skyline in the background.

II *Larry Goldstein*

I *Alex Waterhouse-Hayward*

II *Larry Goldstein*

III *Tom Skudra*

IV *Heather Dean*

I—David Lineker, 38, a pilot with Canadian Airlines, prepares for a flight out of Vancouver.
Lineker, his wife, Bonnie, and their daughter,
Samantha, were thrilled that they all carried the
torch on Day 66.

II—Susan Adair, 45, demonstrates the equipment
she uses as a search and rescue volunteer. Adair,
who became involved in physical fitness about six
years ago, now runs six to nine kilometres each day,
is a lifeguard and swim instructor, and does volunteer work with mentally and physically challenged
youth.

III—Glenn Holstine, 25, is a boom-boat operator
for Weldwood of Canada, Squamish Logging
Division. A husband and father, director of the
Squamish Squash Club, and the head bartender on
weekends at a cabaret, Holstine found time to carry
the torch on Day 67.

IV—James Peerenboom, 14, gets a lift with his
father, a Vancouver helicopter pilot, in Golden Ears
Park, the day before his run with the torch.

I—Husband-and-wife torchbearers Dale and Mandy Crump take a whirl on the dance floor at Dance City. The Crumps, who are in the Silver Program of ballroom dancing, do dancing demonstrations in many provinces and states. They are an active couple: Dale is involved in roller skating, archery and bowling, while Mandy enjoys arts and crafts, fencing and occasional work as a movie extra. The Crumps share presidency of the Goldwing Road Riders Association and have matching Honda motorcycles—dark blue for Dale and pink for Mandy.

II—Catherine Cooper, 75, carried the torch across Vancouver's Cambie Bridge with the help of her grandson Colin, 15. Confined to a wheelchair by a stroke, she writes, "I can't think of anything more special than the two of us carrying the torch together as a team."

III—Anita Wong, 22, practises her craft of ceramics at Emily Carr College of Art and Design in Vancouver, where she is a third-year student. Wong grew up in rural Cloverdale; that background and travel overseas have helped to form her aesthetic as an artist, and also motivated her to apply to be a torchbearer.

II *Larry Goldstein*

III *Kharen Hill*

Jurgen Vogt

William DeKay

Marthe Love

Jurgen Vogt

William DeKay

William DeKay

William DeKay

Just before Hope, the relay began the climb into the first of the mountain ranges that run the length of British Columbia. In B.C. it went through some of the most spectacular and dramatic scenery in Canada, such as the Nine-Mile Bridge near Boston Bar (opposite). In the cities and small towns of the province's interior—Lytton, Spences Bridge, Cache Creek, Savona, Creston, Cranbrook— happy, excited crowds met the relay.

II *William DeKay*

I—Enrico Dobrzensky, 41, has found sanctuary from his hurried life as a businessman in Vancouver on a 6,000-hectare ranch near Cache Creek. The overseer of the ranch, Dobrzensky is perhaps not a typical cowboy —he speaks six languages, has a doctorate in political science, and is a former diplomat. But the ranch is his version of the Canadian dream: "If you think of what Canada is all about, this is one of the most true and fulfilling dreams you could think of." A believer in the Olympic motto of participation, he was honoured to carry the torch, to be a part of the relay in this "modest but highly significant manner."

II—Barry Martin, John MacDonald and Bob Gyurkovits all work at Cominco's Sullivan Mine in Kimberley, and they all bore the torch on Day 79. At the massive mine, which is one of the world's largest producers of lead, zinc and silver ore, Gyurkovits, 37, is the foreman for the team of MacDonald, 36, and Martin, 38. The two, who are brothers-in-law as well as friends, are partners who work underground drilling and blasting—one of the most physically difficult, dangerous and demanding jobs in the country.

I   *Jurgen Vogt*

II   *William DeKay*

III   *Jurgen Vogt*

IV   *Jurgen Vogt*

V   *William DeKay*

VI   *Paul Little*

I—Torchbearers Les Armstrong and his son Wade, at a favourite fishing spot on Kootenay Lake.

II—Ed Bay, 59, reminiscing in a 1929 Argyle dining car at the Cranbrook Railway Museum. A retired superintendent for C.P. Rail, Bay ran on Day 78.

III—Ena McKay, 76, still hunts moose in the hills around her Kelowna home, and keeps active with prospecting and visiting people in rest homes. Her mother taught her to shoot, on a gun that was given to McKay's grandmother by outlaw Billy Miner.

IV—Paul Strukoff, a third-generation Doukhobor, lives in Grand Forks, where 40 per cent of the 5,000 townspeople are of Russian descent and Russian is taught as a second language along with French. Paul's ideals of peace and involvement were well served by his run with the torch.

V—Rossland's Nancy Greene Raine, 44, with her parents, Robert and Helen, at Red Mountain, where she began the skiing career that won the hearts of Canadians and an Olympic gold medal in 1968.

VI—Margo Blackwood ran at Fernie on Day 79.

he rest of Canada is familiar with the famous B.C. triumvirate of disabled cross-country fundraisers—Terry Fox, Rick Hansen, Steve Fonyo—but it has no idea of the number and variety of those who, when the weather turns good, hit the road with a goal in mind. Some do it to make a name for themselves; some do it for philanthropic reasons; some just do it.

There was the 27-year-old man who rode across Canada on a unicycle. A 68-year-old Sidney man pushed a wheelbarrow from Victoria to Ottawa to raise money to establish a home for senior citizens and the mentally handicapped. A 56-year-old woman from Coombs walked across Canada to raise money for the blind. Innumerable people from B.C. have pedalled to Ottawa for peace, and 27 B.C. senior citizens bicycled from Victoria to St. John's for the exercise. Living on the geographic edge, British Columbians feel the need for the centre, and strike out for it by foot and by wheel.

The Olympic flame and its cross-country passage complement this obsession nicely. In Vancouver, one of the torchbearers was Rick Hansen, the British Columbian who wheeled around the world. Hansen went to superhuman lengths to bring the handicapped into the mainstream of society, and pushed hard to have disabled sports recognized in the Olympics. This year in Calgary, disabled skiing will be included as a demonstration event. One is the consequence of the other, a sequence of events that started at home as an idea, and occasionally found fulfilment on the world's roads. One of these roads led all the way to Calgary.

— *Pete McMartin*

Derik Murray / Peter Murray

I   *Jurgen Vogt*

II   *Frank Vena*

I—The first ceremony of Day 79 drew large crowds at Jaffray, just east of Cranbrook. The next day the torch would be carried across the border to Alberta, on the last leg of the journey. In B.C., people thought of ever more imaginative ways to share the Olympic flame. Day 72, in Kamloops, the mayor lit a candle from the flame and took it home to light the pilot light on his furnace, keeping the symbolic warmth of the flame in a most concrete way.

II—Rhonda Lynn Szulc, 29, had the dual honour of being a torchbearer and winning a draw to be the torchbearer chosen to fly to Greece for the lighting of the flame. Szulc described her trip as thrilling, but felt equally excited about running with the torch in Peachland—especially when her husband and one-year-old daughter came up on stage with her and her daughter reached out and touched the torch. Szulc has shared her experience by giving talks to numerous school groups.

III,IV—Some people shared a hug, some people shed a tear. Others yelled, laughed, reached out for the torch, applauded and sang. The Olympic flame touched and moved a nation.

III *William DeKay*

IV *William DeKay*

TO A GLORIOUS BEGINNING
Alberta, Day 80—88

Frank Vena

When the Olympic flame was lured from Grecian skies, the people of Alberta had already been waiting for seven years. Finally, the torch itself—tangible and warm, rather than a mere symbol—was on its way home, to the Olympic Games in Calgary.

From the very beginning, Albertans had made an intense commitment to the flame. During the torchbearer lottery, they assaulted Petro-Canada service stations en masse, submitting hundreds of thousands of applications. Of the 88 days of the relay, 54 had at least one Calgarian running.

Even while preliminary logistics were being considered, the citizens of Fort Vermilion—a small community north of Edmonton—heard of the plan. Their town wasn't included on the original route through the province, but they wouldn't take no for an answer. They lobbied organizers to reconsider, as a nod to the community's 200th anniversary in 1988. In the end, Fort Vermilion was awarded a date with Olympic destiny.

The residents of another Alberta town also showed the Olympic spirit. At Airdrie, the last overnight stop before the flame's march into Calgary, the relay caravan's reservations fell through a week before the odyssey began. Residents responded by generously opening their doors to relay staff.

Excitement peaked as the flame was ushered through the Crowsnest Pass and across the provincial boundary from British Columbia. Carloads of torch fans—mostly from Calgary—made the 200-kilometre drive to towns like Brocker and Coleman, to cheer on the caravan as it began the last leg of its journey.

For Albertans, the Games began the moment Canada took custody of the flame in Athens on November 15. And though they had shared the Olympic flame with all of Canada, they secretly believed that, after seven long years and three road-weary months, the Olympic flame was home—where the heart is.

—Tom Keyser

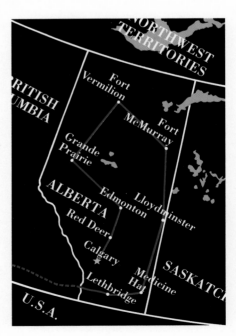

William DeKay

I   *William DeKay*

II   *William DeKay*

V   *William DeKay*

III *Paul Little*

IV *Paul Little*

The relay threaded its way across southern Alberta, through small towns and farming communities, on the final few days before reaching Calgary. Pioneers quickly saw the range, originally the preserve of buffalo, as an ideal place to raise cattle, and huge ranches sprang up. Today a variety of agriculture thrives throughout the region.

I—Scott Holtman, 15, is second in command to his father on their ranch, Shoe String Ranch, near Taber. Scott had to turn down his own chance to run a kilometre with the torch in Saskatchewan because he was unable to travel there, but he made it to the ceremony in Taber.

II—Troy Thieman, #17, and his friends in the warming hut at an outdoor rink in Medicine Hat. Troy, 16, was a torchbearer on Day 73.

III—Raymond Crosschild (right), the last torchbearer on Day 80, with his basketball coach, Marvin Yellow Horn, at Brocket.

IV—In 1969, Wally Bertrand and his wife, Audry, started a small egg farm. Today he happily shows off the produce of La Poulet Poultry Farm, southeast Alberta's largest egg-processing plant. Bertrand, 52, said of his run, "My adrenalin has never been so high since the day I got married."

V—Michael Cowley plays the pied piper as he rolls out a bale of winter feed for his herd of cows. The Cowley Ranch is located in one of Alberta's most scenic areas, near Twin Butte, with the Rockies for a backyard. Cowley is very active in community affairs and sports, and applied to be a torchbearer, in part, to say, "Ranchers jog too!"

I William DeKay

The relay passed through southern Alberta, before circling through the north in a series of flights. From Medicine Hat, it skipped to Lloydminster and Fort McMurray on Day 84, then to Fort Vermilion, Grande Prairie and Namao on Day 85.

I—Beating the odds in the torchbearer lottery, all seven members of the Gillespie family of Calgary were chosen to carry the Olympic torch on Days 76 and 80. But it wasn't just luck—soon-to-be-married Marilynne Heasman and Dr. John Gillespie made it a family project to enter as many applications as possible for the lottery. As David Gillespie, 14, writes, "One night we went to 10 stations in just 45 minutes."

II—The remote community of Fort Vermilion is "the mouse that roared," bending a national event in the direction of a small, proud town. Two years in the planning, residents turned it into a big event: over half the population of about 1,000 welcomed the flame to a 12-metre-long snow stage constructed entirely by hand with shovels. Plans to bus in 2,000 schoolchildren from the surrounding area were foiled when temperatures plummeted to minus 47 degrees and the buses stopped running, but undaunted, the townspeople were still "very jubilant."

III—In Lloydminster, Day 84, Rae Fountaine motored with the torch.

IV—Elsa Hon greets the flame in Fort McMurray, where offices, schools and banks closed down to share the Olympic spirit.

II *Paul Little*

III *Paul Little*

IV *Paul Little*

II   *Larry Goldstein*

III   *Larry Goldstein*

IV   *Tom Skudra*

I—Once or twice a week Jerry and Marian Bayrak get out with the Alberta Rhythm Cloggers for a night of squaredancing in their home town of Edmonton. Jerry ran near St. Albert on Day 86.

II—Hugs and highjinks were trademarks of Olympic mascots Hidy and Howdy at every stop.

III—Jim Hunter, 34, master of ceremonies for the relay, had almost come to the end of a very long road. After emceeing hundreds of ceremonies from coast to coast at all times of day and in all weathers, he was now less than 150 kilometres from the final goal. Hunter said, "I feel like I've been in a Broadway musical that's been a smash success."

IV—The oldest torchbearer of the relay, Calgarian Joseph Chase, celebrated his 101st birthday the day he ran with the torch in Edmonton. Chase has retired three times—at age 62 from the gas company, at 70 from the Department of National Defence and at 75 from General Supplies. His secret for happiness is to "always look forward to tomorrow, never backward."

I *Jean Becq/Andrew Bako*

II *Patrick Morrow*

I—Poised on the edge of the Calgary Tower's top deck, about 180 metres above the city, torchmakers Ron Gibbar, George Henson, Ed Kormyl and Dick Hiebert hold the torch they crafted for the relay. With photographers Bako/Becq, they braved minus 50 degrees Celsius for this unique portrait.

II—Brad Robinson rappels down frozen Cascade Waterfall at Cascade Mountain in Banff. A geophysicist, 28-year-old Robinson was a volunteer at the Winter Games, as well as a torchbearer on Day 88.

III—Douglas Hoffman, 36, sent in over 7,500 applications to be a torchbearer. Torchbearers were very imaginative in their choice of practice torches—ranging from hammers, irons, pipe wrenches and toilet plungers to Hoffman's elaborate "rock torch."

IV—World Cup downhill skier Dave Irwin airborne at Banff. Four of the original "Crazy Canucks" ran with the torch on Day 83—Jim Hunter, Steve Podborski, Dave Irwin and Ken Read.

III   *Tom Skudra*

IV   *Tom Skudra*

Calgary, Day 88

Larry Goldstein

You touch the torch; it touches you.

In the winter of 1987/1988, seven thousand Canadians carried the Olympic torch across their country to Calgary. Some sprinted, some walked, some rode. Some paused to light the candles of those who bore witness to their journey. Some lingered with the torch, savouring the Olympic moment, and others hurried through the cold. All had their own kilometre of Canada and six or seven proud minutes when the Olympic flame and the Olympic spirit rested with them.

—*Michael Farber*

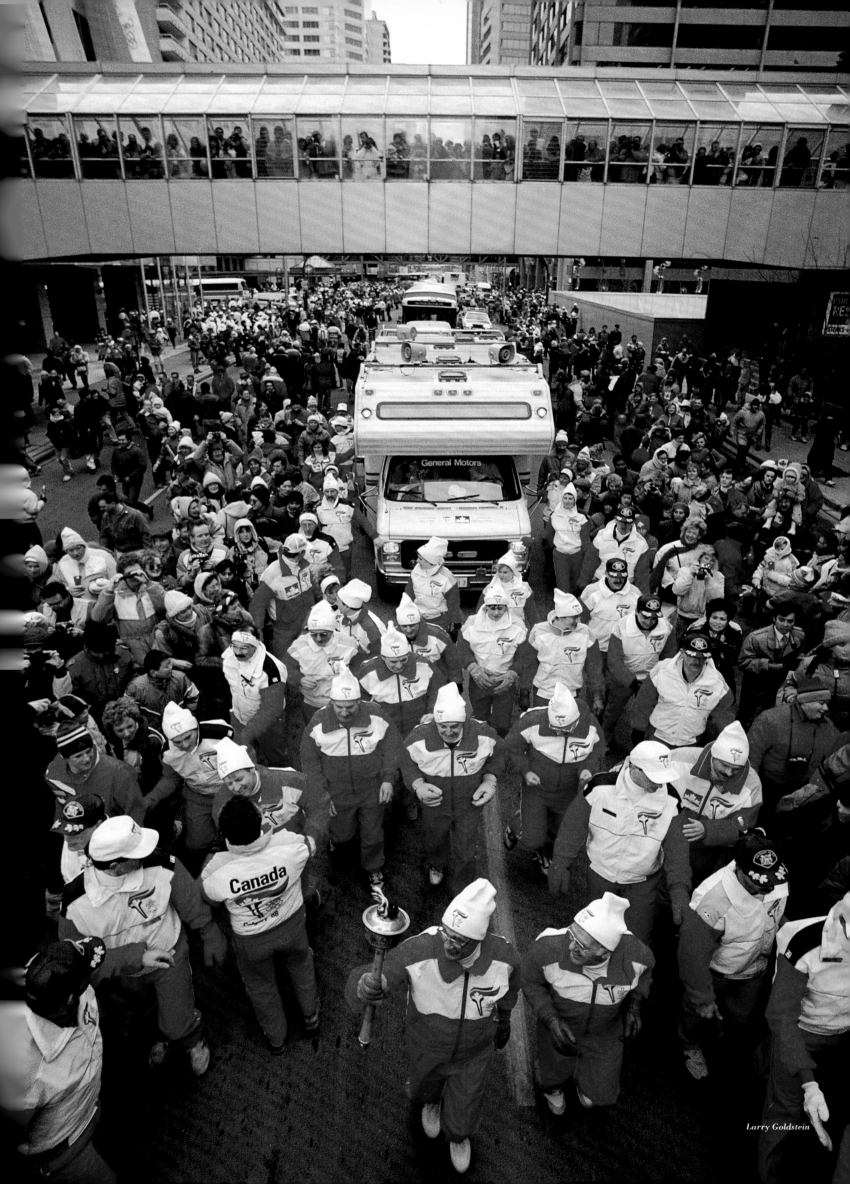

Larry Goldstein

Paul Little

Finally, the torch was home. Its Canadian odyssey had started on November 17, 1987, and it ended on February 13, 1988, when it arrived in Calgary to a tumultuous and triumphant welcome. Over two hundred thousand people jammed the streets, sixty thousand waited in McMahon Stadium, and two billion more watched on worldwide television. Eighty-eight torchbearers from across Canada, one for each day of the relay, joined the lavish opening ceremonies before the torch entered the stadium. It was carried by two Calgarians: World Cup skier Ken Read and speed-skater Cathy Priestner, an Olympic silver medallist. They circled the stadium, stopping once to greet Rick Hansen, then, in a surprise move, handed the torch over to the final torchbearer, 12-year-old Robyn Perry, for the last few steps of its long journey.

Paul Little

Smiling all the way, Robyn bounded up the stairs to the stage. To reach the rim of the giant cauldron, she had to stretch to the limit, and for one agonizing moment, it looked as though she might not be able to reach. Suddenly, with a roar that reverberated throughout the stadium, the flame caught, and the crowd erupted into a standing ovation. In that first spark, the Olympic flame that had touched the hands and hearts of Canadians was passed on to the future.

The lighting of the cauldron has simple significance. At the moment it is lit, the spirits of the ancient and modern Games are united. For Canadians, in this year of the XV Olympic Winter Games, this link had an added importance. On its journey across the country, the torch had ignited the Canadian spirit, and on that Saturday in February, it was joined with that of the Olympics.

Hans Deryk

Jurgen Vogt

THE BOOK – BEHIND THE SCENES

Men Wanted for Hazardous Journey. Small wages,
bitter cold, long months of complete darkness, constant danger,
safe return doubtful. Honour and recognition in case of success.

In the summer of 1987, Derik Murray and Marthe Love couldn't stop thinking about Ernest Shackleton's famous advertisement that ran in London newspapers in 1900. Shackleton had wanted adventurers to accompany him across the trackless vastness of Antarctica; Murray and Love and their publishing partner, Michael Burch, were merely mounting an expedition to follow the Olympic torch down the highways of Canada. Admittedly, it would be cold—sometimes bitterly cold as the torch moved into the far north—and because it was winter, it would be dark for long hours. There *was* the danger of burnout for a team that would be working from seven in the morning to midnight, seven days a week for more than twelve weeks. But if they achieved their goal, which was to have the book in the hands of readers before the Olympic Games ended, there would be honour in having set Canadian publishing records, and recognition in having created a lasting reminder of an event that had caught the imagination of the country.

As it turned out, the work *was* arduous, and at times seemingly endless. Colds and fevers plagued the four permanent members of the road team, who barely had time to stop for major events in their lives—a wedding, a birthday and a death. In Vancouver, 18 people laboured long days, nights and weekends in the face of inflexible deadlines, shaping the photographs and text into a book. Whatever else it was, producing *Share the Flame* was never, ever boring.

Derik Murray and Marthe Love had formed Murray/

Touring photographer Grant Black

Love Productions in Vancouver in 1985, and for recent projects joined Michael Burch, the owner and founder of Whitecap Books of North Vancouver. Together, they approached the relay sponsor, Petro-Canada, late in 1986. The trio had an impressive track record, having published the phenomenally successful retrospective book of Expo 86, *The Expo Celebration*. Murray was an award-winning photographer and director of TV commercials, whose expertise made him an ideal creative director; Love was a skilled projects coordinator, whose ability to handle the minutiae of organizing had been proven in her work on *The Expo Celebration* and in *Exposure*—an ambitious series of seminars she continues to produce for photographers in western Canada; and Burch was a marketing innovator who had made Whitecap into the largest Canadian-owned producer of photographic-essay books and had, with Murray, masterminded the selling of an unprecedented 140,000 copies of *The Expo Celebration*.

When Petro-Canada's manager of public affairs for the central region, Bill Simpkins, gave his approval in May, 1987, Murray and Love had only five and a half months to organize their expedition. As director of operations, Love sat in on Petro-Canada's logistics meetings. She came away with a clear understanding of what *Share the Flame* had to do to keep its team on the road. With costs snowballing, Murray and Burch found sponsors for supplies and services: film and processing, computers, cross-country air flights, two-way radios and cellular phones, a 23-foot motor home,

Marthe Love, Derik Murray

Alan Hobson

Marthe Love, Bill Simpkins

Peter Murray

a photocopier and fax machines, a 4x4 Jimmy, ski jackets and winter outfits, long-distance telephone and fax charges, and courier services.

Throughout the summer and fall, Murray and Love chose their key people. They already had on their staff David Counsell, who had been in charge of the production of their previous books and would shepherd *Share the Flame* through the printing process; Frank Vena, who would fly in to assist the road team; and Brian Daisley, who would identify and code film and handle requests for photographs from sponsors and magazines. Love, the road team's leader, was to be assisted by Andreanne Ricard. Murray's younger brother, Peter, a helicopter pilot and mechanical whiz, was the technical coordinator in charge of driving the motor home and keeping the complex array of equipment operating. Alan Hobson—a bilingual Calgary journalist and broadcaster, a specialist in amateur sport and a nine-time All-American gymnast—was hired as writer. Chris Dahl, an internationally respected magazine art director and winner of national awards for his work, agreed to design the book. Elaine Jones was seconded from Whitecap Books as editor.

Meanwhile, Love set to work on the multitude of arrangements necessary to keep the road team working out of its motor-home office and eating and sleeping in a different hotel every night. For one solid month, researcher Deborah Hlywka did nothing but book rooms, not an easy task in small towns where Petro-Canada had already made reservations for its 80-member entourage. Scott Wanless researched towns and cities on the route to organize drop-off and pickup spots for the courier.

At the same time, Love and

David Counsell, Derik Murray

Brian Daisley, Scott Wanless

Murray began to seek out photographers. Poring over the cream of Canadian photography books and magazines and drawing on their experience, they came up with 85 candidates. Sixty-three photographers were chosen: eighteen touring photographers stayed with the road unit, two at a time for eight to twelve days; forty-five regional photographers worked close to their homes, with the exception of five special assignments, to Greece and various locations in Canada.

Because pictures of torchbearers at home or work would form an essential part of the book, writer Alan Hobson, editor Elaine Jones, Murray and Love read the biographies of the 7,000 runners, shortlisting those who seemed to have interesting stories to tell or who were representative of their areas. After the final selection, researchers Lauren Hamilton, Paris Forrer, Betty Murray and Joelle Da Cunha telephoned each person, gathering more information for the photographers and setting up photo sessions. Every week of the relay, briefs on the runners and creative photography suggestions designed by Murray were faxed to Love and her photographers.

Concerned that the relay pictures could repeatedly be of a grey highway flanked by leafless trees, Murray, Love and Burch arranged a brain-storming session. Out of this four-day meeting in a Banff hotel came a 40-page document, describing the towns, landmarks and scenery along the route.

On November 17—light-up day—the *Share the Flame* crew, poised on Signal Hill in Newfoundland, wondered if they were as well organized as they thought. Alan Hobson remembers finding the beginning toughest. "For one thing, it all seemed to start too fast out of the gate. On top of that was the anxiety of getting

Suzanne Robidoux

Andreanne and Frank Vena

used to the mechanics of the relay and a production system that had never been tried before." He alternated between covering the relay and taking off with one of the touring photographers in the 4x4 to do the behind-the-scenes stories of the torchbearers. Using a lap computer, he

Chris Dahl

wrote on the go, turning out 1,000 stories and vignettes about Canada, for which he interviewed a staggering 800 people.

Ricard spent her days transcribing photographers' notes and documenting their work, shipping Kodachrome film to Toronto and Ektachrome to Vancouver, arranging couriers for out-of-the-way places, and sending film data sheets and Hobson's material to Vancouver via fax.

Love—dressed "like Michelin Man" in a puffy insulated ski jacket and pants, heavy gloves and boots—supervised the photographers who were capturing the relay at the daily community ceremonies and from various vantage points, including an open-backed media van. She carried two walkie-talkies so she could communicate with Peter Murray and relay officials. Sometimes, she'd hop into the motor home to search ahead for picturesque backdrops for the cavalcade. Always, she kept her Nikon handy—and caught several scenes that made it into the book.

By mid-December, the exhausted team realized they had to pace themselves better if they were to run the distance. The Christmas holidays brought flu and homesickness, and for Alan Hobson, the pain of grieving for a five-year-old nephew who had died on December 20. But the new year was happier: on December 25, Michael Burch announced his engagement,

and on New Year's Eve Andreanne Ricard and Frank Vena were married in Ruthven, Ontario—Andreanne wearing a dress that Frank had chosen for her because she couldn't stop to shop. In the new year in B.C., the crew stopped to celebrate Love's birthday with 20 friends Murray had bused in from Vancouver to Lac La Jeune.

In Vancouver, production assistants Scott Wanless and Brian Daisley coded more than 110,000 photographs, which Murray and art director Chris Dahl sifted for those they would fit into the page formats Dahl had already designed. Editor Elaine Jones matched text to the photographs, condensing the 1,300 pages of copy submitted by writer Hobson. Berni Hastings made up the pages of the book on an in-house computer and input the text in English and French. The French version was adapted by teams of translators—Ornella Caprioli, Christine Frédérick, Micheline Jacob, Diane Ranger—imported from Montreal and headed by Suzanne Robidoux. David Counsell coordinated print production during the day and attended press checks at all hours of the day and night. Meanwhile, Michael Burch prepared his distribution campaign, assisted by partner Nick Rundall in Toronto—who had run with the torch on Day 39, Christmas Day.

The first signature went on the press early in January and others followed continually until late February. Staff learned to function with inadequate sleep and hastily eaten meals, bringing in food as they worked through dinner and long into the night. Each day they juggled the various stages of making a book—slides and stories arrived, layouts and text were created, photo and page proofs checked, and finished sections of the book printed. But the stress of meeting deadlines and working long hours was eased with the excitement of every new batch of images and words.

In a Canadian first, the book was printed simultaneously in Vancouver and Altona, Manitoba—175,000 copies in all. The first ones were in the hands of readers only 11 days after the Olympic flame reached Calgary on February 13, 1988, four days before the XV Olympic Winter Games ended.

It had been a hazardous adventure in producing and publishing, with a safe and successful return.

— *Audrey Grescoe*

Berni Hastings, Elaine Jones

Paris Forrer, Lauren Hamilton

Nick Rundall

Michael Burch

TOURING PHOTOGRAPHERS

From November 17, 1987, to February 13, 1988, eighteen of the country's finest photographers worked through a Canadian winter, for long hours and under difficult conditions, to create this portrait of a nation. The book is truly a reflection of their remarkable vision.

AL HARVEY
This "visual hit man" is obsessed by loaded cameras, asking nothing more from life than unlimited Kodachrome and five square meals a day. Downtime is spent tending stock at the "Slide Farm."

ANDREW STAWICKI
Stawicki, a Polish emigre, won the World Press Photo Award in 1974. Since then he's been part of no less than five *Day in the Life* projects—Canada, America, Japan, U.S.S.R. and Spain.

ALBERT NORMANDIN
From car racing to graphic arts to photography, this award-winning Vancouverite chased his dreams to New York City. There he worked with Jay Maisel before returning in 1985.

TIBOR BOGNAR
After a 12-year career as a jazz/rock drummer, Bognar turned to photography in 1980. Today he is one of Montreal's top location specialists, represented by photo agencies worldwide.

STEPHEN HOMER
Homer's odyssey from small-town boy (Woodstock, N.B.) to big-city photographer includes two 1987 gold awards for photojournalism and writing. He lives and works in Montreal.

MICHEL GRAVEL
Gravel, 52, has been one of the names behind the news in Canada for over 30 years. His photographs have graced the pages of *La Presse*, *Le Devoir*, *The Gazette* and the *Toronto Star*.

COLIN PRICE
Cross-Canada treks are nothing new to Price. As personal photographer to Robert Stanfield, he once did the circuit seven times in seven weeks. Today he resides in Vancouver, B.C.

DAVID SEDMAN
The millions of viewers who saw "This Is My Home" in the Canada Pavilion at Expo 86 are familiar with Sedman's fine a/v work. He has been a freelancer for 15 years from B.C. to the Maritimes.

JIM ELZINGA
When he's not toiling in the investment industry, Elzinga can be found photographing people or climbing mountains anywhere in the world. He led the successful "Everest Light" expedition in 1986.

GREG STOTT
Toronto photographer, writer and filmmaker: "This assignment strengthened my affection for Canadians. We're a spirited people, full of a pride I never realized existed."

GRANT BLACK
Black, 30, is a graduate in journalism from Loyalist College, Belleville, Ontario, and a former "Day in the Lifer." He's won nine press awards in his nine years with the *Windsor Star*.

TOM SKUDRA
A veteran of three *Day in the Life* projects—Canada, Japan and America—Skudra has won more magazine and art direction awards than we can mention. He lives in Toronto, Ontario.

BRIAN MILNE
Best known for his book *Trans-Canada Country*, Milne spent 18 months documenting life along Canada's "Main Street"—expertise that made him a valuable contributor to this project.

KHAREN HILL
Hill has worked in Asia, India and Europe but today she calls Vancouver home. Primarily a location photographer, she has had to succumb to B.C. weather and open a studio there.

WILLIAM DEKAY
Born in London, Ontario and educated at Ryerson, this 25-year-old has had a hand in two *Day in the Life* books—Canada and America. He is presently on staff at a Detroit newspaper.

JURGEN VOGT
Born in Berlin, Germany, Vogt came to Canada in 1952. His first foray behind the lens was for *Time* in the 1970s. Today Vogt works mostly for corporate clients. Represented by Image Bank.

PAUL LITTLE
Leaving England in 1971, Paul wasted little time establishing himself here as a freelance editorial, corporate and a/v master. His images often appear in international markets.

LARRY GOLDSTEIN
When Goldstein says he enjoys shooting people, it's not an indictable offence. A commercial photographer for five years, he is well respected for his editorial and corporate work.

REGIONAL PHOTOGRAPHERS

Canada's top photographers have helped produce a penetrating and affectionate look at a vast country and a diverse people. They have shared with us their intimate understanding of their areas and captured the spirit of Canada and this national event. Five regional photographers were also flown to special assignments: Jim Wiley to Greece; Eric Hayes to St. John's; Gary Fiegehen to Inuvik and Yellowknife; Perry Zavitz to Whitehorse; and John Douglas Kenny to Prince George and Fort St. John.

ERIC HAYES
Nova Scotia
Working out of his passive-solar home in rural Nova Scotia (where it took five years to get a private phone line), this veteran photojournalist is now well connected in the world.

ALBERT LEE
Nova Scotia
Four seasons and 30,000 miles by bus, boat, plane, train, troop carrier, taxi, tractor and rickshaw are going into Lee's new book on China. He is represented by Canapress, Toronto.

MICHAEL CREAGEN
Nova Scotia
This Halifax-based photojournalist previously worked as a cook, filmmaker and scrapyard labourer. He is the winner of two Canadian Press awards and a 1986/87 Nikon International award.

JAMES WILSON
New Brunswick
Based in New Brunswick, Wilson has been shooting professionally for 15 years. His work appears in the permanent collection of the National Film Board and the New Brunswick Art Bank.

ARNE GLASSBOURG
Quebec
Glassbourg claims to have graduated Magna Cum Pauper from the Photography School of Hard Knocks sometime around 1979. Today, acting, teaching and shooting fill his days in Montreal.

ANNA BEAUDRY
Ontario
Proving it really is a jungle in Ottawa, Beaudry spends most days shooting women in boas and leopard skins for Boudoir Portraits. Photos for ads and magazine covers add to her hectic schedule.

JOHN DE VISSER
Ontario
In addition to his magazine credits, De Visser has been the photographic author of several books including *Rivers of Canada* with Hugh MacLennan. He lives in Port Hope, Ontario.

SHERMAN HINES
Ontario
A graduate of California's renowned Brooks Institute, this Nova Scotian has put together a superb series of Canadian art books over the past 12 years. He is represented worldwide by Masterfile.

JOHN REEVES
Ontario
From Pierre Trudeau to Tatum O'Neill, annual reports to Inuit art, his subjects are as broad-ranging as the man himself. Reeves also works as a writer and broadcaster in Toronto, Ontario.

BORIS SPREMO
Ontario
Since his newspaper career began in 1962, Spremo has won over 200 major national and international awards. He has covered drought in Ethiopia, war in Vietnam and love here at home.

GEORGE GOODERHAM
Ontario
Gooderham has been exposing film professionally for 12 years now. A York University film graduate, his unique multi-technique approach to image-solving gives his work a fresh new look.

OTTMAR BIERWAGEN
Ontario
Bierwagen's photography can regularly be seen in some of the world's most prestigious magazines. He is represented by both Miller Services, Toronto and Black Star, New York.

PETER SIBBALD
Ontario
Working in journalistic and corporate markets on both sides of the 49th parallel, Sibbald has been freelancing since 1983. He is a former student of Syracuse University, New York.

EDWARD GAJDEL
Ontario
Gajdel, 30, immigrated to Canada from Poland at the age of nine. He studied art history at the University of Calgary and photography at the Northern Alberta Institute of Technology.

JAMES WILEY
Ontario
Wiley will be working with five other photographers to produce a book on the 1988 Calgary Olympics. He is a veteran of the 1984 Winter Olympics, World University Games and Pan Am Games.

ART TURNER
Manitoba
Turner, a 1986 Sam Award winner, lives and works in Winnipeg. He gratefully acknowledges the support of Leica Canada, which provided him with a "ton of equipment" for this project.

DAWN GOSS
Manitoba
Writer/photographer Goss is a woman of many interests, including Seeing Eye dogs, the subject of a recent article. Some of her images will be on show in the Canadian Pavilion at Expo 88.

DOUGLAS E. WALKER
Saskatchewan
From the high Arctic to the Caribbean, Walker's location work frequently takes him from his Regina studio. His stock photography is sold internationally through Masterfile, Toronto.

TODD KOROL
Saskatchewan
At 22, Korol and his career are just taking off. He is presently on staff at a Saskatoon daily as well as being a member of First Light Associated Photographers, Toronto.

ALEX WATERHOUSE-HAYWARD *British Columbia*
Born in Buenos Aires in 1942, Alex took 32 years to discover he wanted to be a people photographer. Today he fights off attacks of landscape photography by buying postcards.

ALAN ZENUK
British Columbia
Sharing his year between Vancouver and Tokyo, Zenuk travels extensively on assignments. For two years running (1986/87), he has taken first place in the Japan Annual Report Show.

JOHN DOUGLAS KENNY
British Columbia
While a Vancouver native, Los Angeles, New York and Paris have all been home to fashion freelancer Kenny. He is a graduate of The Art Center in L.A. and a former assistant to Irving Penn.

GUNTER MARX
British Columbia
Marx has made his mark in the book world as a major photo contributor to *The Expo Celebration* and as co-photographer on *The Forests of British Columbia*. He works out of Vancouver.

HEATHER DEAN
British Columbia
Favourite subjects for Dean's camera are people, aerials and locations—especially around Vancouver. Her work has appeared both locally and nationally over the past seven years.

PERRY ZAVITZ
British Columbia
Zavitz's "somewhat normal childhood" around London, Ontario was radically altered by three years of formal photography training. Today he's an advertising photographer in Vancouver.

GARY FIEGEHEN
British Columbia
Based in Vancouver, B.C., freelancer Fiegehen is currently in the final stages of producing a book on the Stikine River, one of the last free-flowing rivers in North America.

MARTHE LOVE
British Columbia
Share the Flame project coordinator Love credits the 18 touring photographers with helping her hone her photographic skills. She categorizes her shots as a real "team effort."

PATRICK MORROW
Alberta
Morrow, the adventurer, has few mountains left to climb. In the last 15 years, he has conquered the highest peaks on all seven continents and capped it off with an Order of Canada in 1987.

JEAN BECQ/ANDREW BAKO *Alberta*
This dynamic pair is based in Calgary, but they work on location worldwide, shooting for many corporate clients and advertising agencies. They are partners in Bako/Becq Inc.

Share the Flame would also like to thank the following photographers for their special efforts on the project. Susan Brun, *Alberta*; Derek Caron, *Quebec*; Hans Deryk, *Ontario*; Ed Gifford, *British Columbia*; Warren Gordon, *Nova Scotia*; Pat and Rosemarie Keough, *Ontario*; Ric Kokotovich, *Alberta*; William P. McElligott, *Ontario*; Louise Oligny, *Quebec*; Bill Simpkins, *Ontario*; Hans Sipma, *British Columbia*; Darryl Snaychuk, *Alberta*; Norm Stelfox, *British Columbia*; Nedy Vani, *Ontario*; Frank Vena, *British Columbia*; Mark Vitaris, *Alberta*; Paul Von Baich, *Ontario*; Roland Weber, *Quebec*.

ACKNOWLEDGEMENTS

PUBLISHERS
Derik Murray—*Producer and Creative Director*
Marthe Love—*Director of Operations/Project Coordinator*
Michael Burch—*Director of Marketing and Distribution*

VANCOUVER PRODUCTION OFFICE
Derik Murray—*Producer and Creative Director*
Chris Dahl—*Art Director/Designer*
Elaine Jones—*Editor*
David Counsell—*Production Manager*
Berni Hastings—*Computer Page Makeup*
Lauren Hamilton—*Research Coordinator*
Paris Forrer—*Research Coordinator*
Scott Wanless—*Production Assistant*
Brian Daisley—*Production Assistant*
Dana Ervin—*Comptroller*
Cathie MacDonald—*Executive Secretary*
Wendy Darling—*Secretary/Receptionist*
Betty Murray—*Assistant Researcher*
Paul Wylie—*Assistant Researcher*
Joelle Da Cunha—*Assistant Researcher*
Judy Rudin—*Marketing Consultant*
Scott Mitchell—*Assistant Researcher*
Deborah Hlywka—*Consulting Assistant Coordinator*
Don Gee—*Accountant*
Alfred Field—*Legal Counsel*

ROAD TEAM
Marthe Love—*Director of Operations/Project Coordinator*
Alan Hobson—*Interviewer/Writer*
Andreanne Vena—*Assistant Coordinator*
Peter Murray—*Technical Coordinator*
Frank Vena—*Assistant Coordinator*
Len Townsend—*Assistant Technical Coordinator*
Randy Musgrave—*Assistant Technical Coordinator*

WHITECAP BOOKS
Michael Burch—*Director of Marketing and Distribution*
Colleen MacMillan—*Corporate Coordinator*
Cathy Dungate—*Executive Assistant*
Nick Rundall—*Retail Sales Director*
Jim Campbell—*Fundraising Sales*
Des Cobble—*Fundraising Sales*
Bert Eisinger—*Systems Analyst*
Barbara Eisinger—*Data Input Coordinator*
Frank Claassen—*Accountant*
John Parker—*Fundraising Sales*
Linda Ostrowalker—*Accounts Receivable*
Jan McKay—*Shipping and Inventory Control*
Laraine Vancaillie—*Receptionist*
Alex Vuong—*Shipping Coordinator*
Brian Forbes—*Shipping Coordinator*

CONTRIBUTING WRITERS
Mark Abley
George Bain
Paula Brook
Stevie Cameron
Michael Farber
Dawn Goss
Audrey Grescoe
Sheri Grierson
Elaine Jones
Tom Keyser
Gérald Leblanc
Don Martin
Pete McMartin

FRENCH TRANSLATORS
Suzanne Robidoux—*Revisor*
Diane Ranger—*Translator*
Micheline Jacob—*Translator*
Ornella Caprioli—*Translator*
Christine Frédérick—*Translator*

FRENCH COMPUTER OPERATORS
Raynald Robichaud
Linda Renaud

MAJOR SPONSOR
Petro-Canada

SPONSORS
Kodak Canada Inc.
IBM Canada Ltd.
Canadian Airlines International Ltd.
Loomis Courier Service Ltd.
Xerox Canada Inc.
Motorola Canada
Scamper Canada Ltd.
Sun Ice
CellNet Canada, A Division of Bell Cellular Inc.
General Motors of Canada Ltd.

PHOTOGRAPHIC SUPPLIERS
Berkey Photo Canada Ltd.
Lisle-Kelco Inc.
Nikon Canada Inc.
Quad Colour Inc.
Technigraphic Equipment Ltd.

SUPPLIERS TO THE ROAD TEAM
Alpine Electronics
Best Western International Inc.
Onan International
Sealand R.V. Service Products Ltd.
Simson-Maxwell
Sportif Ltd.

Sincere thanks to the following people who worked on the Olympic Torch Relay:

Yezmina Abbany
Shelley Alcorn
Caroll-Ann Bainbridge
Mickey Ball
Audra Bayer
Sylvie Bernier
Marlene Binda
Cathy Bone
Jean Bourassa
Judy Brandow
Yves Brouillard
Terri Bullick
Carol Card
Chris Carriere
Yves Champoux
Irene Charlebois
Geoff Chow
Rocco Cianco
Steve Cooney
Gordon Der
Elizabeth Donnelly
Rene Dupuis
Jim Dyck
Tom Eason
Tom Everett

Pat Farrell
Bob Foulkes
Frank Fournier
Hazel Gillespie
Andy Gouveia
Wolfgang Gregory
Mike Guinard
Salim Hasham
Dave Hocking
Mark Hoffman
Rosanne Hundt
John Hunt
Jim Hunter
Sandy Hunter
Harley Johnson
Frank King
Mike Komisar
Parry LeDrew
Jeff Luesink
Willy Lypko
Keith MacMillan
Bob Mayo
Maryann Meadows
Donna Melnychyn
John Merrifield
Wes Muir
Sheila O'Brien
Tony Pargeter
Lawrence Partington

Bill Pascal
Laura Patrick
Carole Patterson
Marilyn Pelletier
John Percic
Gary Pickles
Claude Plourde
Raymonde Pommier
Brian Purdie
Ford Ralph
Dan Reynolds
Dave Reynolds
Phil Rix
Bill Simpkins
Rene Smith
Terry Steward
Dorothy Tenute
Ron Tharby
Dave Thompson
Helene Tomlinson
Mike Trenchard
Elizabeth Voyer
Judy Wish
Sam Woodruff
Gene Yackison
All Celebration 88 Community Consultants
  and Coordinators
Mascot Coordinators and Performers
The Drivers of Torch 4 Media Truck

In addition we would like to thank the following companies and individuals:

Lance E. Adelvard
Adobe Systems
Agency Press
Aldus Corporation
Don Armstrong
Jim Baglot
Baker Lovick
Stewart Beresford
Leo Biesche
David Bishop
Bruce Boyd
Mary Bowman
Capt. Sharon Broadbent
Sherann Broder
Peter Burke
Bob Burnett
Jim Burns
Canadian Cancer Society
  Volunteers in Whitehorse,
  Prince George and Fort St. John
Canadian Encyclopedia
Diane Cheyney
Paul Clark
Bill Climie
Shawna Crebs
Linda Davis

Dan Dawydiak
David Demers
MaryJane Devine
Cher Dimen Staite
Isaac Dixon
William Dixon
Carolyne Dobias
Ken Easton
Simon Farrow
Bob Faulkner
Larry Franks
David G. Friesen
D.W. Friesen & Sons
Odette G.-Charbonneau
Pam Gardner
Bob Gillingham
Pam Glass
Maja Grip
David Grubb
Lars Hansen
Larry Hawthorne
Chris Hollis
Barry Hooper
Geoff Hovey
Dave Hunter
Ed Isaac
Theresa Jacobs
Russell Keziere
Chandler Keeler
Gary Keen
Kodak Photographic Press
  Centre

David Lamb
Ted Lea
Jeff Lennard
Steven Leopold
Robb Lucy
Allan MacDougall
George McCarthy
Patricia McFerren
Ev McKee
Cathy McKinley
Tom McNown
Bob McNeil
Darryl McPherson
Brian Marconi
Fleurette Monpetit
Wendy Moriarty
Mr. Muir
Louise Neal
Rob Neumann
Betty Nicholson
North-West Bindery
Ronald Parker
Ken Penner
Franca Perri
Laura Perry
Andy Petersons
Petro-Canada Translation
  Department
Jack Philpot
Cliff Pickles
Mark Piercey
Art Pifer

Pola/Graphics
Richard Prokopanko
Andre Quessy
RCMP
Janis Rempel
Andrew Salvatori
Joe Samulenok
Peter Scarth
Bob Schick
Yvonne Siemens
Vicki Sims
Carol Smith
Charlie Smith
Spar Aerospace
Marty Stack
Rod Steele
Hans Strohhacker
Karen Strother
Susan Terris
Wayne Terris
Mike Tette
Ben Theriault
Brad Thompson
Frank Trivieri
William Turnball
Blair Upton
Vancouver Public Library
Diane Walker-Green
Don West
John Wilkie
Danny Wong
Zenith Graphics

June Ziola
Steve Zmetana

Torchbearers on the following pages:
Cover: Sylvie Bernier carrying the
  torch, Day 15, Quebec
Page 2/3: Summer L.N. Preney
Page 4: Graeme Begg and Anita Lammers
Page 5: Hendrick Plug
Page 10: Rick Hansen
Page 11: Katie Alexander
Page 12: Brenda Lucy

Photos taken at the Vancouver production
office by Perry Zavitz

Maps by Jorge Veloso

Photo credit on page 74
should read Tibor Bognar

The producers of *Share the Flame* would
like to thank the 7,500 employees of Petro-
Canada whose hard work and dedication
turned the Olympic Torch Relay into an
exciting chapter in Canadian history.

NELSON · ELIZABETH J MCLAUGHLIN · JAYSON M OLIVER · TIM J SITTLER · DEBRA ANN Y SITTLER · COLIN W TAYLOR · DIANA L TELFER · DARRIN J WHALEY · MARGUERITE A ADAMS · PETER K AFMAN · PATRICK MURPHY · PAUL O DIFONTE · ROBERT H BURBANK · JOHN J CODERRE · ANDREW J DALGLEISH · RONNIE L BURBANK · MELISSA L HARRIS · RONALD O DOUGLAS · RICHARD J GREENFIELD · LINDA HOFFER · DAVID R JONES · CAROL L LEPAGE · DAVID J MCCONNELL · WILLIAM H ROGAN · JOHN F RUPCIC · SCOTT C SHERIN · BRIAN E VAUGHAN · JANICE E AUCKLAND · RANDY C DAWDY · BRENDA O DOWELL · STEVEN V GARVIN · DAVID L JOHNSON · WILLIAM H MAHU · JENNIFER J MORROW · JODY L BROKENSHIRE · JEFFREY L GRAY · BONNIE J HITCHMAN · JEREMY M SNOW · MARION E JONES · DEANNA LEES · MARIE A MERKS · MARTIN L BENETEAU · LINDA E DONKERS · JAMES J PATERSON · LISA B MULDOON · PATSY A MCGILL · STEVE G SABJAN · JANET L SWAIN · STEVEN C SALMONS · LINDA S RUDOVER · ANISSA K GURCHIN · DONALD R GUTOSKI · MARTIN D QUINN · JAMES A TYSON · JOANNE M DALGLEISH · SHAMIM KARMALI · RICHARD D NEWSON · PETER FAUSSETT · MARK FOFFANO · TONY LILEIKIS · PHILIP HUBER · EVELYN GLOVER · KAREN CRICH · JENNIFER ARMSTRONG · JAY MYATT · SANDY ANDERSON · ANNETTE DROOG · RICHARD C BAILEY · DAY 44 · GRAHAM J BROWN · JULIE S DEVOS · JORGE D MARZETTI · LOUISE A BEATTY · BRADLEY J BERGEY · DWAYNE E COTTEL · NELSEY A TONER · GEORGE H DAVIES · KERRI LYNN WESTERIK · PETER M GIELEN · TIMOTHY M ZSOLDOS · KEVIN A JONES · CATHY M MEZENBERG · ROBERT J PATERSON · LIANA J PURDY · JAMES E REID · BARRIE E THATCHER · IAN B CAMERON · ANNETTE M LE FAIVE · THOMAS A LEFAIVE · ELIZABETH C FOX · WILMER R LACHANCE · JOELLE D GAMMAGE · GARY BEACOM · KARISSA J HENDERSON · TIMOTHY C DEHOEY · DR LAWRENCE MALLOY · JENNIFER L MCMONNIES · JOHN L MORGAN · TERRY D SMITH · BRENDAN W SPENCE · GERALD A SWANCE · JAY J VSETULA · GARY J WRIGHT · DERICK W BULLEY · KAREN F CHADWICK · JAMES L COOKE · ERIC LARS LIEDER · SCOTT R BUTLER · GARRY R COWAN · SALLY J DULONG · ROBERTA B DIBBLEY · MICHAEL GETTY · KAREN D ROUS · ALAN F ROW · PETER J SECORD · CHRISTINA L THOMPSON · GREGORY R WAITES · MARIANNE E BEAUSEJOUR · BRETT M BLANDFORD · MARGARET T BERNARD · CAREY D CONDRUK · GARY J DOWDELL · KENNETH J DUCHARME · JAMES R FORREST · ANDROMEDA S FRANIEL · RALPH G HEPPERLE · SHERI L GRUYAERT · SONIA S IOVINO · TREVOR JANZEN · DWAYNE C ST JOHN · MARY C KAUFMANN · HENRY W LEANEY · CATHY MONCUR · RONALD J MCCONNELL · RICHARD P NEUFELD · DAVE J ORSHINSKY · TYLER J PUDDY · JANICE E RAWLINGS · DIANE M REKO · KISS P STEPHEN · JOANNE SECORD · ROBERT G SUTHERLAND · PATRICIA A SEEWALD · ALEXANDRA M SERADOKA · JACK W SULSTON · ANITA M ZALESKI · FORREST A TAVES · MICHAEL K DUCHARME · DAVID G WAITES · NANCY HOSTETLER · ANITA BAKKER · DENISE DURST · JEAN H SYLVESTER · PAUL BRENT PETTIPIECE · LORI A SNOBELEN · ROBERT W MESSERVEY · DAY 45 · ANNE M GIRARD · MATTHEW A HERON · PATRICIA A TURVILLE · EUGENE W ENDLAND · ANTHONY D CIANFARANI · SONJA M DERIKX · HARRY E DICK · PATRICIA GIELEN · TODD A HALLIDAY · FRANK F HAWKES · DALISA A MCLEAN · JOHN J IATONNA · ANDREA A LABAJ · THOMAS C MAYHEW · EDWARD L MONTGOMERY · CHRIS S PRIMEAU · ROGER J STDENIS · PATRICIA VORKAPICH · LARRY G YOUNG · HEATHER A DOWN · JEFFREY E BALVERT · ROBERT B BORLAND · GRANT A CLARK · DENNIS MARTIN · DAVID B DROUILLARD · KATHRYN A JONES · RENE KIELBASA · DENNIS J DUNSMORE · BARBARA J PATTERSON · KELLY JOHNSON · NATHANIEL J BARNES · TERRY ENGLAND · NICOLE A HARRIS · GUY P JEREMSCHUK · DEAN MORGAN · LARRY G REAUME · CHRISTIAN WEINBERG · ALEXANDER ANDRIAN · PAUL L ARCAND · LOUIS J BOMBARDIER · PAUL J BONDY · DAVID N BOWER · DAVID J BOYCOTT · DAVID F CAPE · FRANK G CARDUCCI · JOHN E CHAUSSE · RANDY A NOBES · PHILIPPE J SEGUIN · JOHN W GIFFEN · TONY M ALEXANDER · CHERYL L GILLSON · DIANE C HALBGEWACHS · HAROLD A WELLWOOD III · PATRICIA A KANALLY · STEVEN M KOKOTEC · RANALD A LADOUCEUR · DARYLL P LALIBERTY · MARY ANNE M MARR · SEAN M MORIARTY · CATHERINE MORAND · JEFF R MYERS · JOSEPH D O'NEIL · JERRY M PIPER · ERIC A QUERBACH · MICHAEL J REDDAM · FRANK W SCHNEIDER · JACQUELINE M GAGNIER · RODNEY G SKILL · CHRISTINE H GALINSKI · SEAN H SMITH · PATRICIA-ANN STANNARD · ROBERT L THOMPSON · DONALD R TOWSLEY · KENNETH L VICKERS · JACKIE REID · WOLF WEINBERG JR · JAMES BENJAMIN J BRAYS · RAYMOND W LESPERANCE · SEAN C WRIGHT · JOHN A WATKINS · DONNA A WEINZ · HENRY GING · CHUCK MAXIM · GREGORY B KONRAD · DAY 46 · DARLENE DUFAULT · KATIE TURNER · JOSH R ANDERSON · DAVID R BOYD · GRETA VAN BEEK · TIMOTHY D BOYLE · CARRIE BROUYETTE · ERIC A CHAMPAGNE · JASON D ANDRUKONIS · WENDY-LEE B BEAUCHAMP · MONICA N CHAMPAGNE · SEAN D COSTELLO · ERIN P CAMMAN · THERESA L DORION · GEORGE F ENGLAND · RICHARD J FOLKERINGA · MANUEL V GAUDARIO · GREG M GILLSON · SCOTT A HOLMES · JEAN-MARC L LACASSE · LOUIS P LACASSE · ANDRE LACASSE · JEFF MASSE · MARY BETH LAMANTIA · HOWARD R LEE · LISA J LAUGHTON · DANIEL M MANSELL · SUSAN J THIBERT · KELLY L MARKHAM · VICTOR B MAURO · KENNETH T MCMILLAN · JAMES G MORAND · CHARLES G MORAND · MARGARET E MURPHY · ALLEN DUSHMAN · ROBERT PADOIN · ELIZABETH A PARSONS · DOUGLAS W RAPKO · NATHALIE N PLOURDE · GLEN J REAUME · DEAN S REAUME · BARRY N SNIDER · CHARLES R MAASKANT · JASON N PERCY · CHRISTOPHER M PISTAGNESI · WILLIAM B MCKAY · MARY ANNE M VICKERD · JACQUELINE A BROWN · DEAN P HORNICK · REBECCA A HUNTER · BRUCE E JACKSON · JOHN A LAFRAMBOISE · MELISA D RUSSELLO · H MICHAEL BURRELL · HOLLISTER F DOLL · ROBERT A HARRIS · BRADLEY J WALKER · LISA A GRABEC-DOSKAS · LINDA A DOYLE · CHRIS N MOYNAHAN · LARRY O'CONNOR · LIANA J MOORHOUSE · GEORGE F SAMMUT · REBECCA M MCCLELLAN · CHRISTINE G SCHRAM · LISA C PINSONNEAULT · ALBERT PITRE · JOEY W TONKIN · MARY J SYMONS · MARIE C MCCRAE · JOE O'MALLEY · VALERIE COSENS · PATRICK HILLS · SUMMER L N PRENEY · SUSAN K LAWSON · ROBERT MCMILLAN · JOAN V STANG · B PHILIPPE COYNE · ANDREA RAY · BRUCE GAMMIE · THOMAS GERVAIS · DAY 47 · RONALD W BODNAR · VINCE J BRYDEN JR · DAVE A LAMOUREA · SHARRON E HUXLEY · PATRICK MORAN · SCOTT D PATERSON · TOM OVEREND · ROBERT E TOPLIFFE · DION P BILLETT · RONALD J BULLEY · WAYNE A COATSWORTH · STEVEN R CULP · ELDA M FERREIRA · LLOYD J FOURNIER · DOUGLAS J FREKER · WILLIAM E GUEST · EUGENE J GUILBAULT · STEVE M HASKELL · STEPHEN L HOOPER · MYRE L LESLIE · MATTHEW D METCALFE · MICHAEL S PENNER · BRIAN L HOADLEY · JEFF ALLEN · STUART J SUTTON · SHARON R WIERSMA · BRENDA J WILLCOX · GORDON K CARROLL · SHELLEY L CONLIFFE · KATHERINE A SHERRING · JUDY M HAGAN · ALVIN H KRAAYFNBRINK · INGRID M DEKIEVIT · KA-YU LAW · BRIAN J MCCORMACK · HAZEL M SCHOFIELD · ALAN D RABIDEAU · KAREN R SIMPSON · LINDA H WATSON · BRYAN W WATSON · LAURA L DRURY · WAYNE D ALLEN · LINDA D CHALMERS · DAVID G CAREY · PATRICK R DEMETER · JACQUELINE L JACKSON · GERALD W VAN DECKER · DAVID J DELL · JOHN H EDGAR · MARYANN EDGAR · BRADLEY P EDLINGTON · CHRISTINE A GIANNANDREA · MR FRANK G HIGGINS · TERRY L HAMMOND · FRANK E LUMLEY · SHELLEY R GROSS · PATICIA L HOGAN · JAMES MARTELL · NICOLE J MCKINNELL · JAMES P NAGY · JAMES R PETTIT · HENDRICK C PLUG · KENNETH ROY · JAMES S SMOUT · ELLEN M LUKUSIAK · JAMES R WEBB · PAUL A CARD · BILL PLAIN · CLAYTON C MACNEIL · SHERRILL A MARTIN · IAN M PEER · NANCY E NUGENT · BRENT B FLOOK · CONNIE J MILLS · MARGARET J WOOD · JEFF PERCIVAL · DENNIS ROBINSON · TREVOR J TRISTRAM · JENNIFER L RAAYMAKERS · JOSEPH C WORONIUK · HEATHER A FREER · PHIL MATHIA · SCOTT MANSER · GISELLE MATHIA · HEATHER MANSER · DAY 48 · SUSAN C BURTON · STEPHEN S LIGHTFOOT · TRACY C FELL · TIMOTHY J SAMPSON · CHRISTOPHER P REGIER · JUDITH E WATT · KEVIN A BAGG · HELEN ROSS · ROBERT BELMONTE · MARY J BROWNLIE · LAWRENCE F DEMAEYER · JEFFERSON W GREENAWAY · DANA G MACKINLAY · TERRANCE J MILLS · JANICE A STRAUB · PETER R SCOTT · STEVEN J BARCLAY · JOHN H BRYANS · MICHAEL P BRYCE · JOHN M JAMIESON · MELANIE N RECKER · EDWARD A KESKINEN · MICHAEL J CHESTER · CHRIS DAW · SEAN A MORTON · WENDY K SPRINGETT · BRIAN T CLEAVER · CYNTHIA L MOORE · BRIAN J MACLEAN · JEREMY M FUNAMOTO · JAMES R GREEN · MARK E HORD · KARL R LOEB · SAMANTHA A BRITNEY · RICHARD G ABEL · RALPH V BALDWIN · BRIAN K BATY · DEBORAH E BELTON · FRANCIS R BAUER · STEPHEN K BRIGHTON · KATHARINE J BROOK · BERNARD D CONWAY · LUCY H BROWN · DEBORAH S ETHERINGTON · SHAWN F HANNON · KEITH R FERGUSON · CHAD D FITZSIMMONS · DARLENE SUZETTE NAPONSE · JUDITH A FLANNIGAN · DANNY J FRANK · JOHN D FRIZZELL · MARC P GALAN · MEREDITH A GARRETT · GINA M GERWATOWSKI · KIM ALLETSON · TED F GRZYWNIAK · KAREN GUILD · JULIA M HALL-HOLLAND · TERRI L JENSEN · ELSIE A VAN DEN HEUVEL · KEVIN W HODDER · DAVID T KENNY · EDWARD E KINBERGER · JEFFREY A KLOOSTER · JOHN G KOREEN · ANDREW R LANE · DIANE J LANG · GERRY L LATOUR · CAROLYNN J LANKIN · TANYA D MACCUSPEY · GORDON D MACKINTOSH · NEIL A MCLAUGHLIN · ALISON J MOORE · ROD L PARKER · DONNA A NEWTON · MARC PLANTE · WILLIAM G PRAUGHT · DAVID T RIDEOUT · KRISTYN M SIDDALL · BUDDY C ROWLES · LORETTE F SAVAUGE · JOHN WELLS · JENNIFER GRAHAM · JULIE ARMSTRONG · JENNY BURGESS · LINDA L WILSON · CHRISTINE TEIXEIRA · DR SHIRLEY VANHOOF · DAVID K SOWERBY · TAMMY THOMPSON · PAUL A TATAY · BOB WEILER · MARSHA D VAN ROOYEN · STEPHEN F CONNOR · DAVID A ROUND · DEAN M SIMPSON · DAY 49 · DONNABETH SWEETLAND · MARTHA E TEMPLIN · NORMAN E BIDDLE · THERESA A BARBER · STEVEN R CRAIG · ANGELA R ARNETT · PATRICIA ARMSTRONG · DAVID W DOWNER · DEANNA L CALVERT · DAVID R GRASSIE · LIANE MARIE CREIGHTON · GRIEMENS T DOLORES · CARL HIEBERT · MICHAEL M HAYMAN · MAUREEN KIRKLAND DOW · BILL HEWSON · LORI A DEROCHIE · DONALD G HOPE · BONNIE S HIGH · MICHAEL W MARSHALL · ELIZABETH J KUBETZ · GEORDAN C PATTERSON · RAY S PATY · BILL T SIMPSON · SHERRI E WANAMAKER · BARRY W WILCOX · JEFFREY D WISHART · AUDREY M GRAHAM · DOUGLAS W GULLONS · TERESA A HOWARD · DAVID D MULLEN · DIANE T DELLER · JOHN M O'CONNOR · SHANE K VAN ALLEN · MICHELLE CORBETT · TRACY M BATES · DOUGLAS ALLAN · JEFFREY A LEBOLD · STEPHANIE R DAY · DOUGLAS L BELL · KIM WILLIAMS · DARREN J BIRCH · EARL EHGOETZ · TANYA M DEAVILLE · CLARE G AUGER · DAVID HOLLINGWORTH · RAYMOND A BAUER · JONATHON M BERGHAMER · MARIA L BORGES · BOB FORHAN · KAREN BOERE · JOHN C TAYLOR · MICHELLE L CULP · PAUL M DOUCET · JOHN C EASTLAND · ROBERT G HALL · BRIAN R HILDERLEY · HANNAH L KING · VLADIMIR W KOLAR · CHRISTINA B KRAENZLE · TOM E LESTER · BRADLEY B LEHMAN · MICHAEL WEST · RAINER C MUELLER · JENNY STECKLEY · DANIEL B ROBINSON · KATHERINE L SCHMIDT · WALTER B RAGULA · WILLIAM E BURKE · JEFFREY L CLARKE · STEVEN R SKILLINGS · LISA M MCPHERSON · DANNY G JOHNSTON · CATHERINE A MOSCALL · BRIAN G DEAN · KENNETH G CORMACK · CHRIS STRAHM · ERIN WHITE · BRIAN PEDERSEN · GEOFF STUBBS · DEB ZELLAS · DAY 50 · ROBERT P BRAZEAU · RONALD SCHIAVO · LAWRENCE G ABEL · BRYAN H BROOMFIELD · LISA D CHARIE · JAMES J CAMMAERT · LEE-ANNE M D'AOUST · NORMAN M FINKELBERG · SONYA DROUMTSEKAS · HARRY I GHOSH · CORIN B DEBRUSK · AMY C FINCH · RALF GOETZE · TIMOTHY P DIEBEL · KIMBERLY J ACKERNECHT · ALLYSON J HAGGERTY · JOSEPH A DUNHAM · BRENDA L KARN · STEVE W MARTIN · JENNIFER L KAY · FREDERICK J MCLACHLAN · MARY JOAN MCKEEVER · MICHAEL J MEDCALF · NIKOLA M MEHES · TRUDY L NOVAK · MIKE J MURDOCH · JOHN C RICHARDSON · CHRISTOPHER P ROGERS · CHRISTINE FACEY · GARY A BYRNE · MARGARET R ROYDS · TONY SALAJKO · KEVIN D SHANTZ · GARY K SMITH · MAUREEN L SZUCS · FRANK R VOLPINI · DIANE THOMPSON · DEBORAH A TAYLOR · TERRY W WATASZKO · RUBY WEBER · CHERYL GIBSON · RICH C WELTER · KATE E WHALE · CHARLES K BONTJE · RUSSELL M CULLINANE · RICHARD A MCCLEARY · CATHY L WALLACE · WILLIAM G MCNAB · JULIE M HAMILTON · ERMINIO OLIVERI · MARY J LYNCH · DOUGLAS J SPINKS · KAREN L JOHNSON · GEORGE R PERRY · DAVID M ALVES · SHERRY L DAMMEIER · REGINALD F RIDLEY · HEATHER J HALLMAN · DONALD T KIRKPATRICK · SONJA B VAN DE HOEF · DALE C BARBOUR · MICHAEL J BRIGHTLING · VALARIE VANDE KEMP · KEVIN F COWARD · DEANNE L BAYKO · DAVID G HABKIRK · RICHARD J LANDRY · TERRY D MCLEAN · ROBERT W OLMA · HEATHER F SEARS · FREDERICK TIESMA · STEVEN W WATSON · MARIE-HELEN JOLY · CECILIA C SBRIZZI · JEAN-MARIE PEPIN · BRENDA L ERNST · LAURA GIFFORD · PHILIP ZIEGLER · NEIL MUNROE · ROGER TERNAN · CHRIS MCFARLANE · DAVID IRWIN · DARYLL F DAVIES · REBECCA A HARDER · DAY 51 · JEFFREY M KINNIBURGH · GREGORY R MACDONALD · MONIQUE M MACKINNON · BRADLEY E ST CLAIR · MICHAEL J MENZIES · TERRY A BRAMHILL · STEPHEN J ROTHDEUTSCH · ALVIN J CLARK · LISA C KINDREE · SKIP GRANT · JANIE M REID · THOMAS M DEMBIE · LINDA L GUTHRIE · STEVEN M HALKO · ROMAN D HALKO · KARENA E LANDERS · GLEN K HESTER · SUSAN HOLLOWAY · ANDREA M MCCORMICK · WILLIAM S LINKLETTER · RANDY HUTCHINSON · YVETTE L MOORCROFT · PHILIP W PARKER · JEFF THEEUWEN · RYAN L STEVENS · MICHAEL C TRAIN · DAVE J VANSTONE · GORDEN R WEBBER · BRUCE HALL · TAMI E STRILCHUK · CRAIG C HUNTER · PETER NIIT · CATHERINE L SCULTHORP · ROBERT J SCULTHORP · CHARLES D SOUTH · BROOKE C BURNETT · STEVE R MCEOWN · RACHEL A HALLER · MONIQUE C PURDON · DONALD K STANLEY · MICHELLE R VANKOOTEN · FRANK ZAHNT · CHRISTIANNE BANFIELD · BRIAN D LUCAS · WAYNE M MILLER · WILLIAM G IVES · AUDREY J STUKAS · LYNDA P SWAN-MATTHIES · ROBERT J BEATTY · ERIN C THOMAS · KIMBERLEE A GILLANDERS · GERRY J BESWORTH · JOHN H BRAY · DAVID P CONNELL · JAMES L CORMIER · OWEN A DYKSTRA · JAMES W FERGUSON · SHERYL ANN FRESHWATER · JOHN W HALL · NELSON B HARNDEN · MARYANNE L HOGG · WILLIAM J KENNEDY · GARY M LAURIN · WILLIAM R DYMOND · DONALD A SCOTT · JULIE IN PRINCIPE · JAMES E PRICE · TYLER H STRACHAN · LYNDA E ROTONEN · GEORGE W TAYLOR · KEVIN CLOWES · LEEANNE LAVERTY · MONIKA KRAMER · KERRY RICHARDSON · SCOTT MARTIN · ROBERT C THORPE · JOSEPH E LIBRALESSO · DAY 52 · MR FRANCIS MAGUIRE · DARRYL PECK · FATHER MAURICE OUIMET · LEAH A AXT · BLAIRE V BAKER · JIM B BEATTY · DAVID A CARTER · SUSAN M BUNKER · SHARON J KOPCZEWSKI · KATE MULLIGAN · GEORGE MORTON · JOSEPH A NEMANIC · ELLA M SMITH · COLIN H WELLS · WALTER K WELLS · JOHN E BIGELOW · JAMES BROOKER · WALTER P BULAS · ALAN J JOHNSTON · LEONARD A BULL · ANGELA E BUSS · JOSEPH M CANDO · KIMBERLY A CARLSON · GARY A CARLSON · JOHN P GORDON · JASON J IRANI · JENNIFER L SHIPMAN · STEVEN J JOHNSTON · DAVID J MAHEU · BARRY L KELL · ROBERT M KENNEDY · ROBERT S BEL · ROGER D L'ESPERANCE · BRUCE C MCKAY · ALLAN R PAAVOLA · EDWARD E RIDGWAY · JASON J SMYTH · RICHARD G STOREY · ANGELA J WHETHAM · LIISA SAVIJARVI · MICHAEL J TRACE · ELIZABETH A LIPPERT · MICHAEL P OSMANN · SARAH J BEARCROFT · KATIE A LEXANDER · WILLIAM D PEARCE · HEATHER A POTTER · BARRY W AULT · ROBERT C BARROW · HUGH A DORE · RICHARD L FULFORD · TIMOTHY B JOHNSON · MARIANNE C LOCKHART · PAULETTE C BRIGGS · ROBERT G MATTHEWS · RONALD P FRASER · ANGELA J LAMIRANTE · JOANNE VALIN · MICHELE MARKLEY · THOMPSON E CLINE · SHAWNA L CLINE · NANETTE R FOX · JOHN R LETTS · ANN HEMPHILL · WILLIAM T PAYNE · THOMAS R GOUGH · DAY 53 · LAURA BUSKO · BRENT K SCHRINER · JACQUELINE L FEQUET · GEOFFREY W DIXON · CHAD C BROUGHTON · DONALD C BROUGHTON · MAURICE CHARLEBOIS · ERNEST M GUMMER · JOHN SEGUIN · WANDA M LAWHEAD · MICHAEL MCCORMICK · CHERYL A O'NEIL · TIMOTHY A ROCHETTE · SHARLEEN D PIOTTO · FRANCIS PENASSE · JACQUES R SARRAZIN · CRAIG H SLATER · MICHAEL J WESTLEY · CAROLYN D LABRECQUE · TANYA MARIE NESTERENKO · JOHN A THORNTON · KENDRA SHEPHERDSON · STACEY L GOBBO · ROD A MACKAY · CHRISTOPHER E MACK · DOUGLAS F MARCON · LOUINE B MCCALLUM · CHANDA L OLIVIER · GEORGE M BRAKE · SUSAN M BOWERMAN · JOESPH BUKATOWICZ · BRUCE G CLARKSON · SHERI L GAZZOLA · FREDERICK G HENNING · JAMES H IRVINE · DEREK S LAHNALAMPI · JOHN C KENNEDY · LARRY D KENNEDY · MICHEL A LAFOREST · DANNY R LAMOUREUX · CHRISTOPHER E LEFROY · PETER STANKIEWICZ · TREVOR J LESLIE · PAUL W MAKINEN · TIM E MALLETTE · DANIELLE M MALO · BOUNO MANARIN · ADELE A MANNILA · MICHAEL E MORRIS · RICHARD J MOSS · CARL E NOEL · TINA LUISA PIETRANDREA · SAMUEL F SMITH · RAYMOND R ST-HILAIRE · THOMAS J STOTT · JULIA E SULLIVAN · GILLES G THERIAULT · JULIE J YOUNG · DAVID E WHITE · GREGORY A WILSON · STEPHAINE L LAWSON · G L BUDAVARI · SCOTT E MARTIN · FRANK R NADEAU · LINDA M SCOTT · ALEX BAUMANN · NEIL M HENNESSY · MICHAEL LEBLANC · CHRISTY HYNDMAN · SHANNON S KENNEDY · JASON KING · CHRISTOPHER CARAPIET · PHILIPPE FARMER · MARC ROWE · LEAH YOUNG · DALTON M RUSSELL · THOMAS HAIGHT · SEAN SCOTT · SALLY J LESK · TRACEY LYNN T GROTTOLI · ROLAND PORTELANCE · DANIEL C MICHAUD · GILLES T DERIAULT · ANDREW CHAPADOS · DAY 54 · ALAN J BALLAK · STEPHEN M CADY · EVAN C EVANS · MARTIN M LABBE · CHRISTOPHER W LOCKMAN · GREGORY V NADEAU · TRACY MYRNA TOULOUSE · ROCH M GAUDRAULT · ROY MEAWASIGE · LAURIE A KENDRICK · JOHN R CAMPBELL · ERIC C STEWART · JASON K WOODS · BRADLEY C BADELT · JIM CADA JR · ELIZABETH M BARBER · CAROLYN M BARNES · LISA JEAN BELEC · ROBERT C DONALDSON · VALERY M CATCHPOLE · PAUL R BERNARD · JUDITH MARIE HORRIGAN · DAVID S HALL · JOHN E GRANDMONT · FRANK FATA · RAYMOND J EBERTT · DOUGLAS J KING · RYAN J VLAAD · MARGARET L DEFAZIO · JOHN ROSE · NATALIE LUCILLE JEWETT · JOHN C PINE · DONNA L KREZEK · JEREME T YOUNG · LAURIE KREINER · RAYMOND R HURTUBISE · MARK O KIRK · ARTHUR J SHANNON · DANIELLE L BOUCHARD · CAROLE I HARE · DANIEL C LACROIX · KRISTA L KOMMUSAAR · JANE L MAITLAND · STANISLAW MASZCZAKIEWICZ · MAUREEN A KUNTZ · KATHLEEN A MARSHALL · MICHAEL C MARSHALL · JAMES M MCLEAN · ALBERT A PIHLAJA · TOMMY G PORTER · DEBORAH L STEVENSON · LAURIE A STEVENSON · RICHARD D THOMAS · JANET M WOHLGEMUTH · ROBERT J WORKMAN · JOHN A MARRIOTT · DAY 55 · RHONDA L CASE · INGRID J BROWN · BADELT C BRADLEY · GAYLE L DAVEY · HENDRICUS M VAN DENZEN · CURTISS R NYSTEDT · CHRISTOPHER D BEMROSE · RUSSELL E MASON · CAROLINE J DUKES · ALISTAIR M MELVILLE · DAVID M MCLEAN · ROBERT J MONARCH · STEPHANIE JONES · WILLIAM D NASH · DAVID M DUCETTE · PAUL A ORAZIETTI · RICHARD C TELFER · CAROLINE C DUBREUIL · JULIE M PALLOT · ROBERT J ZUFELT · MORLEY S MOSSING · REGIS A O'CONNOR · BILL ALLAN · DORY E DERESKI · DARYL E DERESKI · DARREN C DICKSON · JOSEPH A GALLO · RONALD G HALE · JOY-LYNN C HATFIELD · HENRY F HECHLER · SANDRA L KEITH · ALAIN L MORIN · PAMELA C O'HEARN · TARA-LEIGH O'HEARN · AMBER L ROBINSON · CAROLE L STYRES · PAULA J PILON · GILBERT J SABOURIN · ELEANOR DIANNA BILUK · DAY 56 · DONALD J DONAIS · PATRICIA L KOZLOVICH · GERALD J ROTAR · JOHN C SHAW · BRENDA L BELL · JAMIE C BOSLEY · DONNA L DUGUAY · GORDON V WOROSHELO · DOUGLAS P ADEY · JACQUELINE A DERESKI · GERALD M DONALDSON · CHRISTOPHER J GLYNN · AGNES M IWANCZYK · LAURENCE H SIMONS · GERALDINE A TURNER · DONALD G BENO · ROBERT E MCKINSTRY · MICHAEL D ADAMS · THEDA CAISSIE · GEOFFREY B DAVIS · ORIAN L HARPER · ROBERT M ORLOWSKI · ELIZABETH M JOHNSTON · DANIEL M PEDWYSOCKI · SHERYL S KUSHNIER · WADE P ROONEY · JOANNA L LARSON · FRANCIS GOODCHILD · KENNETH M SHIELDS · SUSAN E MAYES · RAYMOND J MACISAAC · TREVOR T TUCKER · LES WILLIS · GEORGE ZURAWSKI · DAN COLES · SHELAGH MAUREEN BASHER · DAY 57 · PATRICK J CURRIE · ANDREW J LANKTREE · NICOLE R CLARK · CHRIS J CLARK · SHIRLEY F BOUCHER · THOMAS A CHANDLER · KENNETH E COMMISSO · GEORGE P FESNAK · BENJAMIN C FORS · BARBARA A BRITTON · PATTI A GESSIE · RAYMOND H HOGARD · JOHN C HARGREAVES · WENDY D AIKEN · ERIK B ALLEN · CURT R ALLEN · DOUG KYLE · GLEN H HARRIS · DAVID R HARRIS · MARLENE J HEITLAND · JEANNE L HOGARTH · RICHARD O IRRGANG · JOANNE A HULSE · ANDREW JACKSON · ANDRE E JOLIN · KATHRYN L KIMPTON · R D KIMPTON · MIKE KOSKI-HARJA · GILBERT L LABINE · DANIEL M LAGACE · HOLLY E LAWRENCE · YVON LEBEL · LISA A LEMIEUX · DENNIS W MARTELL · DIANNE L MCNICOL · MICHAEL E OBERT · KRYSTYNA PERRON · JOE W PALAHNUK · RONALD N VOPNI · THOMAS WARREN · HALVORSON N GLEN · SHARON A WISEMAN · TERANCE P YAKIMAK · TAMMY L ZUREVINSKI · DANNY J BROWN · EDITH J RAMANATHAN · THOMAS S DAWES · WAYNE R LAGACE · MURRAY D LARONDE · JON A MATSON · GLENDA J MYERS · CORINNE A WYNALDA · KENNETH H WASHBROOK · DAY 58 · KAREN M SEELEY · BRIAN K BEREZOWSKI · GWENN A BODIE · WILLIAM J BOWMAN · ROBIN L BOURDEAU · DAVID A BUZZI · JANET A DAVIS · WALTER B CHAPMAN · PAMELA E DAWES · JAMES L DORRANCE · JAMES J FITZPATRICK · ERIN L GORRIE · GLENN A KRUGER · BONNIE J LLOYD · THOMAS D MCCULLOCH · STEPHEN E MOYSEY · KATHY A PARADIS · ALLAN J POIRIER · VANESSA M STAFFORD · WALTER STECKY · KATHLENE S VIBERT · MARGARET R ALLAN · E ORVAL GOULIQUER · SHELLEY A BENSON · BRUCE A HOSSACK · ANNE R HOSSACK · ALEXANDER D MATIECE · L TIMOTHY THIESSEN · DONNA J BRUNTON · RENATO A CARBONE · GARRY V LAPWORTH · HENRY H MILLER · TIM DONKERSLOOT · ROBERT W STARRATT · DEBRA G ROY · DAVID P MUSHQUASH · TANIA O LEGROS · DONALD HAINS · TED HAINS · HEATHER K CHAPMAN · FERGUS F CHAPMAN · ROBIN M DAWES · JOHN B LAKE · LORRAINE GUSTAFSON · LAURENCE DE MARCH · DAVID M MOUSSEAU · ALISON M OGDEN · GUNNAR W WIKANDER · TODD WALLIN · W ROBERT POILE · ROBERT TRUTHWAITE · JOSEPH GALLIKER · LAURIE J HAYTON · KEN FORD · R NEIL KEATING · JENNIFER ANNE GOVIER · LEE F DONALDSON · DAY 59 · SHERRY LEE FAST · KEVIN B JONES · CYNTHIA D CONE · DAVID G GROFF · NATALEE-JO WIHNAN · KEITH J MACFARLANE · GLADSTONE F BLACKMORE · GILLIAN M KING · DANIEL J LOHR · JENNIFER L TINSLEY · PUAL J HOMIK · LESLEY-ANN HARTSHORNE · RUSSELL J DEW · ROSE BULLEY · JOAN E ATKINSON · ROD M KUENEMAN · SUSAN D GEDDES · WILLIAM G GRABOWSKY · AMANDA C HYWORREN · PATRICIA M GARRITY · MARK S OXER · BRANDEE J ALEXANDER · MATHEW COLLINSWORTH · ANGELA L ENFESTY · JANELLE RUE · DONNALEE R DREBIT · DONALD MICHALSKI · YVONNE MYAL · ALLEN M LEVENEC · DIANE T KEAM · CLIFFORD E POCKETT · COLIN M FLEMING · SYLVIA JENSEN · TOM S SCERBO · DOMINIQUE M NAYET · KIRSTIN J SWANSON · RONALD D OSTHUS · BRIAN J PIERCY · DAVID E MCCAIG · GORDON J NICHOLSON · NICHOLE T WILLARD · SAMUEL G NAYET · WENDY R RALLEY · ALICE J SZARKIEWICZ · BOB MORGAN · BRIAN A SCHIEWE · BRIAN L KESSLER · CRAIG L MCGREGOR · EDWARD M PIETRUSZKA · PAUL CHARTRAND · ANNIKA WEEKS-LINTOTT · CAMERON S WRIGHT · JERIN L STANLAKE · TREVOR J WARKENTIN · DAY 60 · JEFFREY W EASTON · CORINNE M DROBOT · PIERRE J CHEVRIER · DONALD S FLETCHER · ALLAN GREINER · ROBIN JOHNSTONE · YVON J W DUMONT · BLAINE M SENICK · TANIS SHYIAK · ZDAN R SHULAKEWYCH · CAROL M CKINLEY-BENOIT · GERALD P DESMARAIS · PAULETTE M DESMARAIS · LEO G BLANCHETTE · DAVE MATEUSH · MONIQUE A RENAUD · THOMAS B DOBSON · ELEANOR A GAIDY · JIM A MELNYK · HEATHER L STASKA · LORNE FERLEY · SARAH E BALODIS · LEONARD RATZLAFF · PHILIP A SCHAIBLE · FRANCIS H HANLON · PETER WILLIAMSON · BRANDY A CATTON · C JEAN BRITTON · KEVIN R CHATWIN · DOREEN A COST · DONALD K TERANISHI · JOCELYN A MILLS · KORY N SENIUK · CAROL D DUPRAS · BRIAN W ELLIS · HEATHER L JACKMAN · SHERI T GOULD · DONALD W THIBIDEAU · DWAYNE F WASYLENKO · H PAUL GILBERT · JANICE A KENWORTHY · TIM A KLUMPER · GABRIEL A LEPAGE · TRACY LEIPSIC · JOHN MCKENZIE · MIKE SIRANT · DOUGLAS G PISTAWKA · RAYMOND B JONES · ADRIANA M NAROZNIAQ · DARCY F LYTLE · KEVIN L LEWIS · TAMARA EWING · DENNIS J MARK · MARYBETH MAHER · HENRI P POTIER · GLENDA L FRASER · ROSEMARIE L PELOQUIN · DANA L TOROSSI · RANDALL E WILLIAMS · FRANK WINKLER · MARG M WEDLAKE · MICHAEL D DICKSON · KIM T WEBSTER · GARY A HANSEN · GEORGE M MACK · GEOFFREY S WILKINS · TAMMY J SWITZER · JUSTIN M LUCH · DAY 61 · FRANK DERKSEN · IAN B GREAVES · PAUL J BURGESS · CRAIG J HABERMAN · BRENDA L CANTIN · TIM MCISSAC · RICHARD J ELDER · EUGENE M WARWARUK · CHERYL C SORENSON · DIANE RATNIK · ANDRE J GOBEIL · SARA N MULLER · TERRY G CABLE · MATHEW A GUSTAFSON · RONALD J BELL · ALISON WHITAKER · DONALD J HUTCHINSON · PAMELA C KOWALCHUK · KAREN F LESCHYSHYN · STEVEN MAKSYMYK · FRANK R MARTENS · SHELDON L CAMERON · JEFFREY N MOYER · FRED J MURRAY · LAINE J SAUNDERS · HARLEY SHUSTER · THELMA J BROWN · LEANNE T MCDONALD · EDWARD J PETZ · KATREENA C WILSON · JIM W GOLDING · LARRY DOAN · BRENDA L HUCKELL · HUGH STRENDIN · DOROTHY PELLATT BODE · BARRY W BRODA · GREGORY D COOPER · JENI HORNUNG · RICHARD J TOFANI · LINDA CARLSON · DAVID J HUGHES · FLORIAN J SOBLE · LAWRENCE W CLARK · STEPHEN FOX · CARMAN BOSS · STACEY J REEVE · ROCHELLE A THOMLINSON · GARY MILLWARD · DONOVAN HOCKLEY · KENNETH MITCHELL · KEITH J COLLINS · KIMBERLEY QUINN · TARALYNE AKERMAN · SHANE DOREY · NICOLE T GLEIM · ALANA V GIBBENS · RAINA N BROWN · DAY 62 · CHRIS J ANGELL · ADELARD L DOUAN · KENT D LANG · DONALD H HULL · DEBRA L BAZARSKI · AARON A BENKO · DONNA M PLAUNT · RICHARD E KROGSGAARD · MARK B FOGEL · AUDREY J VAIL · H DOUGLAS RAMSAY · DEBRA LYNN NEDELCOV · HENRY J JOERISSEN · SCOTT LEITCH · PATRICIA L BARRICK · DWAINE J LAR · WAYNE MCKENZIE · CELESTE A MORSE · BRIAN GROCHOLSKI · YVONNE M BACHIU · PHILIP W BARCHARD · PAMELA L KRYWULAK · WAYNE A CALDER · JENNIFER M ENGLISH · BRYDIE C BETHELL · RICHARD K LEACH · RICHARD ONG MARK · DIANE TAM · MARK T THIESSEN · TAFALINE D WALL · TODD G WALZ · BRENT FRANK · COLINS B GEBER · W JAYE MITCHELL · STEVEN C SAGAL · CHRISTEL SCHOLTEN · MARILYN CAMPBELL · TERRI LYNNE SMITH · LORNA J ANAKA · DAVID L SPETZ · TERRY D GERGELY · MICHAEL G POWELL · JAMES G RUDACK · ROBERTA L REYNOLDSON · RICHARD R SIBBALD · GRAEME R SMITH · PAMELA R KRAUSHAAR · JASON D BODNARYK · STEVEN J BRIERE · JOLENE D FOSTER · ALLAN E ABRAHAM · JANINE DAUNCEY · REIM HIGAZI · LORNE M HUNTER · KEN THOMSON · JACINTHE M ASSELIN · DAY 63 · PAUL MEHLSEN · JOCELYNE M PAQUET · CYNTHIA N READ · CHERYL W READ · CHERYL D LYONS · KIMBERLEY A MARSHALL · MARK T HENDRY · TRINA L LUBIANESKY · KEITH M WILSON · MELANIE M EREISER · KURT M BRESHER · HOLLY L FLETCHER · BRUCE W HERGOTT · LYNDA C HARRINGTON · DAVID J CALLELE · RICHARD D BROKX · JUDY M LUCZKA · SANDY G MCVITTIE · DIANE F OKRAINETZ · FARLEY KELLETT · CRAIG MACKAY · DOROTHY M GEORGE · STEVEN M SILVERNAGLE · DWIGHT R SHANNER · TRENTON S JOHNSTON · ROBERT G SEMENOFF · MARY-ANN VERLINDEN · TREVOR E PFLEGER · JEREMY D WEIGEL · KIRBY W BOYCHUK · S CRAIG FISHER · TARA R CUSTER · LEONARD V LAPRAIRIE · WILLIAM J PACHOLKA · DONALD R PANCHUK · GLEN TROWELL · ROBERT M SYMCHYCK · DALE S POLISCHUK · GERALD M STONE · APRIL A VICZKO · HALEY N STEWART · STEPHEN R BLES · PETER F BERNARD · COLLEEN L KIRKHAM · RODNEY L BUCHAN · JAYSON S HEADRICK · ERICA A BUTTON · JAMES P HERREM · TREVOR J BELSHER · CINDI J CLARK · DONALD J SIGNORI · ANITA TKACHUK · BILLY J DUPRE · SHERRY L WATT · CLAYTON L LANDRY · SHIRLEY J KRONE · COLIN A GOSSELIN · DANIEL H BOBOWSKI · CHARLENE NIEMAN · JOEL WILKINSON · LISA NIEMAN · JAMES F HUDSON SR · D. ALLAN SILZER · DAY 64 · RAY J BRAZEAU · NEILL A THOMPSON · MARK S EVESON · KAREN LEGRESEY · BRAD S LAUZON · BRENDA A FINLEY · TODD H HARKNESS · BOB LAUZON · KELLY A MUIRHEAD · ANN L LATIMER · ANDRE J TRICOTEUX · NORMAN SANGRIS · LORNE A SMITH · SHARMALA R BUELL · DONNA M JOHNSON · KENN SMITH · DALTON E DALIK · VERNA FIRTH · JANICE A NIKKEL · LYNDA GERRY · IAN ORBELL · GRACE E LOREEN · STAN RUBEN · VICTOR DEMKO · BARRY COOK · FRANCIS C SEGUIN · VICTOR A BOTARI · RITA D PASICIEL · JASON R PAGE · LORRAINE LOKOS · PETER JOHN MATTHEW MAYCOCK · BRADLEY C JONES · STEPHEN CHARLIE · PETER R WILCOX · WILLIAM A BENNETT · TOM FAIRMAN · DIEDRE K DAVIDSON · MICHAEL B BOLAND · WENDY E CHISHOLM · JAMES BOYDE · JANET M ARNTZEN · PAUL J MALLOCH · ARLENE L YEULET · GERRY A STOCKLEY · ALAN TAYLOR · RON MCFADYEN · JAMIE L PETERSEN · WILLIAM H RIVERS · PAUL C SIPPEL · DAY 65 · PHIL M ASHER · BONNIE G BAILEY · DOUGLAS E DEAN · KELLY J FORD · TYLER KEDDIE · NICOLE L SCHMICK · CINDY A SIMPSON · CHARLES REID · KERISSA M DICKIE-BALL · DONNA J BULMER · GRANT E SPELSBERG · PATSY A SWENSON · JACK L REDKOP · ANGELA D RAPPEL · LANCE J OLLENBERGER · RHONA E MACDOWALL · JASON W LEXA · JENNIFER D KOZMENIUK · GORDON M CRAMP · LORI A VAN BOUREN · LINDA M JOHNSON · JAMIE R BIRK · MARGARET F HARDWICK · TIMOTHY MUSTART · KATHRYN HANSEN · MARGARET A SURINAK · LAWRENCE W CLARK · LINDSAY A CLEMENTS · NEIL J CONNOLLY · TARA L DANIELSON · JOHN W BIRD · GAYLE K FLINTOFT · JASON C MARZINZIK · SUSAN M PEETERS · SIDNEY A ROSS · CARRIE L PAHOLKA · FRANCIS H BLUES · SHERRI L BOCKING · WESLEY A CALDWELL · MECHELLE M MCMORROW · GORDON J OLAFSON · FRANK C BROWN · SIDNEY MCKNIGHT · BRADLEY E CALYNIUK · ROBERTA M LANG · SCOTT TWERDOHLIB · LISE A GALL · JAMES A SWEET · KIERA M CLAUGHLIN · BRADLEY T EZELYK · MICHAEL J DORAN · PAUL FAKE · WERNER HOOGE · LOUISE C MCGUIRE · ARYN J HANSEN · NORMAN E HOOPER · DARYL G JARVIS · IAN P MOONEY · JASON SEAN PAUL NEAULT · LEE S PENDERGAST · MIREILLE N ROLLMANN · ZEB KING · GARY F V BURGESS · AARON D CABLE · BILL JOHNSON · JASON D'LEWIS · JANET M OGG · ANTHONY HOYLE · STEFANIE R HORSFALL · MICHAEL H HENSHALL · COLETTE N IDIENS · ALEXANDER B STUART · MARK D WHALLEY · DARLENE G HOBENSHIELD · F BRIEN DOLAN · MOYA FRISCH · ASHOK K BHANGER · DIANE E ECCLES · GLADYS C DICY · JESSE D DICY · DOUGLAS A DICY · YVONNE J BIRCH · KARIN M AUSTIN · ROY A BICKELL · JACQUELINE A COHOON · MICHAEL A BROOKS · SHANE W FERGUSON · JANINE L FLINT · CHRISTINE A MACCASKILL · ROBERT D DAVIES · SHAWN C FEARING · BOB MILONE · RAE M SMITH · AVRIL SOKOLOWSKI · MICHAEL D WALKER · BRIAN D MATTHEWS · WESLEY LOGAN · RICHARD D KELLER · ANDREW M KAJDA · NICK HOEKSTRA · BRUCE C HOBSON · DAPHNE E WILSON · MIKE A GALLOP · HANNAH L SHOOP · JOE J EDGINGTON · LESLIE MACGREGOR · TYLER G CHANDLER · ANNE TIPPETT · MELISSA FLINT · LAURIE MCLEOD · JAMES COONEY · LAURA J FORIN · ROBERT T NOLLAN · LYNDA M FYFE · JAMES A MCPHAIL · SHAWN M ROBSON · SUSAN G VALDAL · DAY 66 · CARLA BURTT · JEFFREY S LLOYD · ZETA M RAMIER · THOMAS V HEAD · TERESA D ROBSON · RICHARD G DACK · KENNETH THOMAS LANGEVIN · STACEY M KERKHOFF · DENIS E KABUSH · BONNIE L LINEKER · SAMANTHA K LINEKER · DAVID G LINEKER · NORMAND ROUETTE · PATRICIA V MCAFFER · EUGENE P MILES · SONIA G TOOKER · ANDREW G MORRISON · COURTNEY M MCMILLAN · BRENDA M LUCY · DAVID A COVERDALE · WENDY LYNN CRAIG · CELINE M FORAND · HUGH MCDOUGHT · MR N WILLIAM BRINGMAN · SUSAN K DUNBAR · LUCAS J ST CLAIRE · SHIRLAYNE DENNING · COREY J GAUNT · STEVEN N DELVES · NEIL S FERGUSON · KATHERINE A HENTGES · JOHN A HENTGES · LORI A HITCHCOX · BEN S MAARTMAN · MISS KERRY F KENYON · PETER C GEDDES · MARION A LINDBERG · BROOKS W LEHTONEN · ELIZABETH MOORE · GEORGE LOEPP · PAULA D SCHINDEL · NORMAN S MARSHALL · BETTY L STEVENSON · GENE C MCPHERSON · JULIA F TUNER · ALSTON M MILLER · KATHERINE FRANK · FRED BOB · KATIE BOB · GEORGE HARRIS · ANGELA WHITE · ARTHUR C NESBITT · ROBERT L WRIGHT · KENNETH WARREN · SAUL D SPEARING · AARON M STOKES · FRAN FOWLER · THOMAS A SMILLIE · PETER J RYDING · JEAN E GRAHAM · MICHAEL J BALDWIN · PATRICK J BRAND · CHARLENE S CORRIN · KEITH H DOMINA · SUE J PERELL · MICALYNN B THOMPSON · HOWARD KELSEY · JULIE A RAYMER · LEANNE M DOUGLAS · DOUGLAS G RUSSELL · AMY C JUNG · CRAIG MCCONNELL · MS CLAUDE F POUMEROL · PHILIP M MCCORMOND · MELISSA A KNOX · JOANNE E O'CONNOR · ROYSTON A PREVOST · EDWARD H SAMUEL · RONALD F HEAL · TYLER C HEISTERMAN · WALTER E KROEGER · DAVID J MCKAY · BRENT MACTAVISH · JAMIE LUND · ROB BORTOLOTTO · TODD CREED · FRANK W NASH · BENJAMIN R WALTERS · LEWIS T KAMANN · GARY A VAN DOORN · DEBBIE L BROWN · BEN A DESCOTEAU · SHELLEY L GOODWIN · DAVID F MOORE · DAVID JAMES RUMMEY · GERALD W STEELE · JANICE MASON · DARRIN C PLAMONDON · ROBIN J PEARSON · IAN A WILLIAMS · VERONICA M LUKASCH · ANDRE MELYNK · DEBRA M MANULAK · LEGER JOSEPH J COURTEMANCHE · JENNIFER M POST · TRAVIS W MERRIMAN · ANNE L SHERIDAN · SASCHA B WILLIAMS · JUDITH M COULTER · ERIC N OLSON · DAN J SULZ · DAVID R DENIS · CHRISTOPHER G IVERSON · MARILYN D MORRIS · IAN C PHILLIPS · LYNN E BRYDON · WALDEMAR BIERNACKI · CLARE CHARLOTTE CRONIN · MARK BROWN · WENDY L DAVIES · KENNETH F CLOW · THERESA A HARRIS · TREVOR D FAWCETT · HEATHER M HARRIS · ALLEN S GLEDHILL · MARK D FOREMAN · MARY-LOUISE STACEY · LANCE S HASTINGS · DONNA L LARSEN · GLENN S HOLSTIN · LORENA MCCALLUM · MURRAY A JAMES GROOM · DUNCAN W KIRKPATRICK · LEE A PEACOCK · SEAN DENNIS MARSHMAN · STEPHEN J SAFAR · TOM B BREWSTER · DAVID A LOEWEN · JARRET V OLSON · PETER J EASTICK · NEIL J NEWTON · GORDON A PRILL · JEFFREY D NASH · BRYAN W LUDWIG · JAMES A LAUDER · WAYNE E GRAY · FRENERICK PLEASURE II · KIMERLY ANNE SKEATES · JAMES S AINEWORTH · ROSS ATKINS · DAVID A ROSS · WILLIAM CRAWFORD · DALE ORTON · GLEN A ALLEN · CHRIS GUSS · DARREN KENNEDY · KEVIN ROBILLARD · BOB BEHARREL · SCOTT PAZIUK · WALLY BZDELL · MIKE ZIMMER · MICHAEL BIGGS · DAY 68 · CHARLIE G CUNNINGHAM · MAREA J NELSON · PETER M SIMKIN · COLIN J BEXSON · LYNN A CLARKE · GRAEME D BEGG · ANITA J LAMMERS · JOSEPH JEAN ROGER BOIVIN · TRYNTJE HORN · DEAN CRAWFORD · PATRICK TURNER · CARL MOENCH · MARY E PARTRIDGE · RON J COLEBORN · LOUISE A DE LUGT · CHRISTINA M SHEPHERD · ROBERT H PERRY · MIEKA J VANDONKERSGOED · MINDY D ARCHER · RICHARD L CHARLTON · GWENDOLYN E LOCK · RICHARD H PETERSEN · MICHELLE B HOLDSWORTH · CHARLIE G COLEMAN · NIKOLA Z ZANIC · CHARLES R YOUNG · DEAN DUBE · SHEPHERD D JOHNSTON · LORNE W MACKIE · DOUGLAS TOSH · KENNETH G HORNE · MARK A MARES · DONALD G OLSTEAD · CHRISTOPHER W RICKETTS · AARON S HASSON · CHRISTOPHER J ROYCE · PETER L WESTHAVER · BRYON R MACGREGOR · JILLIAN D OLSON · MONICA K MCCULLOUGH · VALERIE J WILSON